DEMYSTIFYING CANCER

EXPOSING THE DECEPTION OF THE 'NO CURE' FOR CANCER

Devon S J Morgan

TruthSeekers Publishing

Published in the United Kingdom by
TruthSeekers Publishing

E-mail: healthtruths4u@hotmail.co.uk

British Library Cataloguing in Publication Data: A catalogue record for this book is available from the British Library.

ISBN 978-0-9569191-4-4

Editorial services by Kwemara Publications

Acknowledgements

A special thanks to Anthony Robbins, life coach, for his 'Living Health' tapes which started the process of my understanding of the root cause of cancer.

A special tribute to the makers of the 'Eating: The Rave Diet' documentary.

I will be forever grateful for the teachings of Dr. Llaila Afrika, the foremost naturopath. His teachings represent knowledge that should be obvious if we apply common sense.

I would like to thank all the people I've quoted herein. Their insight, knowledge and wisdom have enhanced this book, inspired me, and strengthen my understanding of cancer. A special thanks to Dr. Tim O'Shea for his consent to the use of extensive excerpts from his article.

Special dedication:
To my late aunt, Yvonne – Mrs Y E Stacey.
Gone too soon.

CONTENTS

CHAPTER ONE

CHAPTER TWO

CHAPTER THREE

CHAPTER FOUR

CONCLUSIONS

MOTIVE FOR WRITING THIS BOOK

Have you heard of the ridiculous and alarming statistics that cancer will affect 1 in 2 men, and 1 in 3 women in the United States, and that the number of new cases of cancer is set to nearly double by 2050?

These predictions are based on statistics collected by the National Cancer Institute. There are similar statistics that are related to heart disease and the other major diseases. So, my first reason for writing this book is one of self-interest. I have a keen interest in being alive, and being a part of this wondrous earth and universe. As a result of my keen interest, and because of my awareness of the prevalence of diseases, I've developed a fondness for not only living, but also to experience the reality of enjoying a long and *healthy* life. Writing this book has served to strengthen my understanding of how to care for my mind and body. My second reason is also one of self-interest. Having recently lost my aunt to cancer, I would like the system to be better equipped to deal with this dreaded disease, just in case any of my friends and loved ones should also become its victims.

My third reason is based on a desire to add value, and to make a difference in the lives of others. When we were young, we had a tendency to scratch our names together with the date on rocks and trees with the message: "I was here." I think this is because of a built-in desire to be remembered as being a person of significance or importance. It is the expression of an unconscious or conscious urge to leave something behind to mark our passing. If I can save one, or several lives with this writing, then this book would be my mark indicating, "I was here". If you share the contents with one person, or with many and it saved them from suffering and pre-mature death, this book would also represent your mark of, "I was here". If I can make a positive difference in changing the world's approach to ridding us of this disease, my life would be expanded in a unique way.

This book is the result of knowledge I gleaned whilst piecing together information about cancer and about solving the cancer epidemic. This information came from a combination of a wide range of what I call, 'an informal human-team-effort' of mainly doctors who practice both allopathic and naturopathic medicine. It is also the result of analysing information from official and unofficial organisational sources. These ideas were particularly gathered from many of those who thought 'outside the box' and who were not restricted by self-interest, or by the rigidity of their training, paradigm and legal considerations. We are intelligent life, and there is no human problem we cannot solve if we have a full grasp of its basic root. We will only not solve a problem if we have misdiagnosed it. If we do this, we will be forever looking in the wrong direction. On account of the size and urgency of the cancer challenge, we now need a collaboration of doctors and diverse health practitioners to come together in a *formal* human-team-effort to solve this assiduous threat to human dignity and life.

Service to humanity is the best work of life. – Unknown

PREFACE

I think many of us are uneasy about the fact that there seems to be no cure for cancer. I don't mean, here, that we are uneasy because of the fear of getting the disease. I think this unease is rooted in a subconscious feeling that something is wrong because of the absence of clarity as to why we get cancer and why so many die from it. Many have expressed to me their feeling that there is a cure but it is being kept hidden as a result of some conspiracy theory. However, the overwhelming reaction to the prevalence of cancer is fear. In many people's minds it is a big, mysterious, monster killer that is beyond everybody's ability to explain or conquer. So, for many who have been pronounced as having the big 'C', they and their loved ones would go into a panicked lock-down. In this state of mind, logical thinking, practical thinking, and the use of common sense will take flight. They will then embrace the remedial system they have been socialised into believing to be the best available.

They will do this even though this system declares that they have no cure! I think people do this out of some vague promise heard – that chemotherapy, or radio therapy treatment, will extend their life. Yet it is never clear how long they would live without this treatment, or even with this treatment. There is never any clear finality with this approach. After such treatments, the person will live in 'remission', an uncertainty in hope that the cancer will never come back. This is why I often say to people: "The best time to study any life-threatening subject is when you are not experiencing it." In such a scenario, you are relaxed, and at your most resourceful because your mind is not clouded with fear. In a non-threatened state of mind, you can be more objective and reflective. You can then carry out leisurely research, and meditate on the answers you will find. There is a saying that goes, 'if you search, you *will* find', and the answers are surely available for those who would like to understand the nature of cancer, and the best way to avoid or overcome it. This book can be the catalyst for you to research and expand on the answers that I have found. We owe it to ourselves and to those who love us to be able to defend our health. This personal development knowledge is also the greatest gift we can give to those whom we love and care about.

PROLOGUE

We find ourselves on this spinning blue and green planet with free will, and no knowledge of how to live. But at some point in the evolution of our consciousness we have come to understand that we are very different from other life forms in a very important way. We recognise that we have no built-in knowledge of what we should or shouldn't eat. We also need to do *research* in order to find ways of healing ourselves. This does not apply to any other life form. This is an area of our development that we have to make a *conscious decision to study and practice.* Learning how to experience life-long good health is part of our responsibility in having free will. It is also a necessary undertaking if we wish to live up to our claim of being the most sophisticated creatures on this planet. Consciously taking responsibility for the care of our bodies is also vital for the extent to which we thrive, survive and experience enduring happiness. The universal quest for happiness will be impaired if we are ill.

I always encourage people to live life as if they were preparing for a marathon, rather than to live life as if preparing for a sprint. At best, most sprinters will train to have enough stamina for about four hundred metres. However, to live to our genetic capability, in spite of all the poor nutritional choices available, and environmental obstacles, requires knowledge, and a kind of preparation that is conducive to giving us enough stamina and endurance for a marathon. The sprint approach implies less attention to detail regarding what to eat, or not to eat, what to drink, or not to drink. Those who are careless with their diet; those who 'live to eat', instead of 'eating to live', will often have the equivalent of 'a short burst of life', likened to a sprint.

If we are not consuming for the 'distance run' our choices may be based on taste, and less on nutritional considerations. This approach has a high probability of attracting illness and a relatively short lifespan. On the other hand, the marathon approach is based on the opposite. With this we are required to practice a detailed nutritional approach that will nourish the body for stamina and endurance. With this approach we do not use taste alone in deciding what to eat. With it we have a greater likelihood of avoiding the major diseases whilst also living a much longer life with greater vitality.

The marathon approach can be compared to having a goal of reaching the moon. In this scenario there is no room for error. If you miscalculate and miss the moon, you could find yourself in a situation where there is no way back. Life, too, can have a similar outcome. If you miscalculate how to care for your health, you will find yourself suffering the accumulated effect of your daily neglects and errors in judgement. It is true that the body does have a point of no return.

Science has shown that the human body is amazing in its construction. It therefore requires a type of care that is in harmony with the science of how it works. The body has a defence system that is normally adequate in defending it from the natural, foreign matter that forms a part of our environment. The body also has an internal 'clock', and this determines genetically how long we can live. This is what makes us mortal. It is not astonishing that we can live comfortably and healthily to age one hundred and beyond. Most animal can't live this long because their 'clock' will not permit it. A fruit fly will live for only one day! Nowadays, however, in spite of the clear indicators that we can live comfortably beyond one hundred years, it is quite common for the majority of us not to get anywhere near this age. The strange thing about this is, we are not alarmed! Yet, if we observed the same thing happening in the rest of the animal kingdom, there would be an international panic! There is no panic when this happens in our world because of a word that has become our great enemy in the crusade for health: *normal.* No matter at what age people find themselves in poor physical health, this is regarded as a 'natural' or 'normal' part of life. Yet, in the natural world, we observe that animals tend to have greater consistency in their physical condition and duration of life. This is because they eat what they are designed to eat. In other words, what they eat is in harmony with the science of their body.

Free will distinguishes us as humans. It also makes our lives the most challenging. Why? Because nothing is compulsory! We can choose to learn, or not to learn. We can choose to reason, or not to reason. We can choose to accumulate common sense/wisdom, or not to. To compound this weakness in our character, we have developed an education system that is not holistic in its inclusion of essential life subjects. One such subject is health and nutrition. In general, we have an education system that produces graduates who suffer from 'the right hand not knowing what the left hand is doing'; that is to say, they are over specialised. In this situation, most students are totally ignorant of the expertise of others and so rely blindly on those who provide our services. A person could be a brilliant computer engineer, or physicist, but knows nothing about medicine, or about the care of their body, and the same can be said in reverse for the medical practitioner.

The National Conquest of Cancer Act was signed into law by former US president, Richard Nixon, on December 23, 1971. He declared a war on cancer, and promised a cure for the disease within seven years. It did not happen. Do you consider this a failure? Isn't this a classic demonstration of the 'right hand not knowing what the left hand is doing'? In general, do politicians know anything about the practice of medicine? If there had been a doctor who was a politician, *he or she would have been trained to think from the same point of view as those in charge of finding a cure.* He or she would have been thinking from an allopathic point of view. In effect, there was no system put in place after the act was passed to structure and monitor the approach and effectiveness of those whose job it was to eradicate cancer.

A successful cancer treatment is defined as surviving surgery, chemotherapy, and radiation for five years. If you die of cancer in the 6th year, the treatment is still considered a success! In this scenario, age is irrelevant; so, if it were a child, it would not be considered alarming! This surely cannot be the outcome that the National Conquest of Cancer Act was passed for. It highlights the absence of a system that should monitor and measure results in human terms of health and wellbeing.

Those of us who never seek to bridge the gap in knowledge outside of our education and training, especially in areas that can have a life and death outcome, have reduced our power to choose how best to solve such situations. It is a rule, rather than the exception to it, that extremely brilliant people will, in the case of serious illnesses, throw themselves at the mercy of their doctors. They show total faith in the doctors' almost divine right to know what they are doing. This book is an opportunity for you to pause and think about the basis upon which you've accepted the status quo as to what constitute real medicine. It is also a chance for you to question your understanding as to what foods are best compatible with the human body.

At the rate that we are going, in terms of our diet and lifestyles, we are living our lives as if we are playing Russian roulette. Our health status is like a candle in the wind. It is the luck of the draw as to what illness will cause us to die. As it stands, many of us will die from one of the major diseases. It will be listed as 'natural' causes on your death certificate. It is no more natural to die of cancer or other major non-communicable disease than it is to die from a drug overdose.

The greatest danger we face is not guns, knives or bombs. The greatest dangers we face are food and 'medicine'! – **Author**

INTRODUCTION

The science behind the human body is of such a high order that we cannot go into a lab and duplicate it – it is more advanced than our capability for construction or invention. Wisdom dictates, therefore, that we should respect and honour *its principles* and not impose *our standard* on its care. It did not come with a divine 'instruction manual', so therefore we are required to study it, understand it, and then nourish and treat it according to its unique scientific standard. Wisdom dictates, also, that we should comply with its nutritional requirements. To emphasise this point in conversation, I have stated, "If I were involved in the design of our body, I would make it compatible with the eating of many very salty, processed 'foods', because I loved such 'foods'.

From painful experience, however, I discovered that the body does not welcome such choices. This realisation led to the inevitable conclusion that the body has principles or 'laws' by which it functions at its optimum. Therefore, if we break its principles or 'laws' because of our lack of understanding, it will become ill, and we have no other place to 'live'. It was not fun for me to live in a body suffering from pain. The absence of a divine 'instruction-manual', or a 'built-in-programme' (instinct) of how to care for our body, has led to quite a few schools of thoughts which concern how to care for, or how to restore the body to health. The two schools of thought that form the basis of this book are referred to as *allopathic* and *naturopathic* medicine.

THE NATUROPATHIC APPROACH TO MEDICINE

Because naturopaths study and focus on the wellness principles of the body, this philosophy naturally leads them to determine what the best forms of nourishment and treatment are that would be in harmony with the body's understood biochemistry. In effect, the naturopath's primary focus is to determine the most effective ways to maintain, or restore the body to wellness. The following are some of the principles and approaches that are at the basis of the naturopathic approach:

- The naturopaths accept that the body is intelligent, and that its primary drive is to maintain life.

- They therefore seek to determine the following: what is the right chemical balance of the body that is conducive to the maintenance of wellness?

- They conclude that if our body's biochemistry has a pH balance that is slightly alkaline, that this is the ideal state for good health. From this they conclude that the chemistry of fruits, vegetables, and herbs are ideal in maintaining the body's healthy pH balance; or, in the case of illness, they are very effective to restore the body's healthy pH balance.

- The naturopaths conclude that if the intelligent body is helped to restore its healthy pH balance, it is well equipped to heal itself. This is in harmony with the quote from Dr. Isaac Jennings: "There is no healing force outside the body." The naturopaths also conclude that herbs, preferably with little or no modification, are effective in restoring the body to a healthy pH balance.

- The naturopaths consider it inane, and a criminal violation of the Hippocratic Oath (of upholding morality in medical practice), to introduce any 'medicine' to the body that would harm it.

- Cancer, like any other disease, is regarded as the body being out of balance. Their focus is to understand the specific cause(s) related to the formation of the cancer, and then to help the body get rid of that specific imbalance. The overriding philosophy is to return the body to a state of balance.

- Naturopaths focus on a change of diet, lifestyle, and herbal supplements. They embrace the *'your food should be your medicine'* philosophy, and their objective is for the body to be strengthened to the point where it facilitates a permanent reversal of any disease.[1]

Like hunger or thirst, the instinct for balance is built into the human body. – Deepak Chopra

---

1 *There are thousands of cases where people have reversed serious cancers by changing to a strict plant-based diet.* – "The Rave Diet" (DVD documentary)

THE ALLOPATHIC APPROACH TO MEDICINE

- The allopathic approach is primarily focussed on the treatment of diseases, or, to be more accurate, it focuses on the treatment of the symptoms of diseases. For example, a headache is treated by numbing the nerves that are *registering* the pain with drugs so that we stop feeling it. The *cause* of the pain is rarely dealt with. The primary focus is to stop the pain, but the body can actually correct the cause of the pain without painkillers. If the cause is severe, as in the case of migraines, the cause has to be found and corrected, or else there will be a regular recurrence.

- The allopathic approach to making medicine is to significantly modify, or create an *altered or synthesized* version of the natural treatment in a lab, and so create a drug.

- This process creates drugs that are *lethal* enough to be used for suicidal purposes. This dangerous nature of drugs is why we are asked to keep medicines away from children.

According to Wikipedia, in reference to allopathic medicine:

"The practice of medicine in both Europe and North America during the early 19th century is sometimes referred to as 'heroic medicine' because of the extreme measures (such as bloodletting) sometimes employed in an effort to treat diseases".

Allopathy [álopáthē]

Etymology: Gk, *allos* + *pathos,* suffering

A system of medical therapy in which a disease or an abnormal condition is treated by creating an environment that is antagonistic to the disease or condition; for example, an antibiotic, toxic to a pathogenic organism, is administered to treat an infection.

- This 'extreme-measure' philosophy has continued with the treatment of cancer using chemotherapy. Drugs that kill both good and bad cells of an organ, as does chemotherapy, have to be considered extreme.

- The allopathic philosophy regards cancer as a growth of bad cells that must be destroyed by any means necessary. Hence the use of surgery, radiation, and chemo drugs that kill both good and bad cells.

- Cancer cells are regarded as invaders in an otherwise healthy body. The goal is then to destroy these invaders.

- *Strict diets such as macrobiotic or vegan diets do not contain dairy or animal products. This can stop you getting enough nutrients for your body to work properly.* – Cancer Research UK

- It is true that strict macrobiotic or vegan diets may not provide all the nutrients that the body needs. However, dairy and animal products are not the ideal missing nutrients. You will see evidence further on in this book that they contribute to the cancer epidemic.

- Allopathic practitioners are still at the level where they think we need to eat dairy and animal products to get sufficient nutrients!

- There are efforts being made to enable the targeted elimination of cancer cells. If this becomes an effective reality, it will still not eliminate the root cause of cancer. Therefore, if the cause remains in place, the cancer will return. The Ancient Egyptian principle of Cause and Effect will always rule supreme.

- *New treatments need to be compared with accepted and proven treatments within a properly organised series of clinical trials before we can be sure of their true benefits.* – Cancer Research UK

What is meant by clinical trial? A clinical trial is described as, '*a rigorously controlled test of a new drug, or a new invasive medical device, using human subjects.*'

Have there been any clinical trials carried out on the effect of fruits and vegetable foods on cancer? How about doing a trial where some people are placed on a diet of fruit juices and vegetable juices, and compare the result with those who take chemotherapy? Later in this book you will read some information on this point, sourced from the National Cancer Institute. This information may surprise you. It highlights that the current research and medical system needs to change. The fact is, cancer kills millions of people annually; many of whom are high-profile, extraordinarily productive people. One of the most recent notable, high-profile people was the innovative founder of Apple computers, the late Steve Jobs, who was only 56 years old. This disease is, therefore, contributing to a serious brain drain. If the system doesn't change, this will continue unabated.

CANCER IN THE WORLD TODAY

According to the World Health Organisation (WHO):

- Cancer is a leading cause of death worldwide, accounting for 7.6 million deaths (around 13% of all deaths) in 2008, and 8.2 million deaths in 2012.

- Lung, stomach, liver, colon and breast cancer cause the majority of cancer deaths each year.

- About 30% of cancer deaths are due to the five leading behavioural and dietary risks: high body mass index, low fruit and vegetable intake, lack of physical activity, tobacco use, and alcohol use.

- Tobacco use is the most important risk factor for cancer, causing 22% of global cancer deaths, and 71% of global lung cancer deaths.

- Deaths from cancer worldwide are projected to continue to rise, with an estimated 13.1 million deaths projected for 2030.

- It is expected that annual cancer cases will rise from 14 million within the next two decades (Fact sheet N 297, February 2014 updated figures).

The increase in death rate from 2008 to 2012 translates to 150,000 deaths per annum. If this cancer death rate started at the beginning of the nineteen hundreds, the death rate for 2012 would be about 16.8 million. This confirms that the cancer death rate is accelerating at an alarming rate, and will double or more by 2050.

Pause for a minute and have a careful look at the third bullet points above. Now, ask yourself this question: Why would a low intake of fruits and vegetables cause people to develop cancer? After you've considered this question, you should then realise that the statement is also saying that *fruits and vegetables protect the body against cancer*. The 'behavioural risks' listed and how they can also be the cause of cancer will be touched upon later in this book.

According to the International Agency for Research on Cancer, an estimated 12.7 million new cancer cases were diagnosed worldwide in 2008. Therefore, if 7.6 million people died from cancer, this translates to about 60 percent of those who were diagnosed with cancer in 2008, died that same year!

In considering the information above from the WHO, you could ask yourself the following, why don't governments highlight specific foods that cause cancer? What about the WHO? They have already highlighted tobacco and alcohol, but I don't think these are what they are referring to by the term 'dietary risks'. Tobacco and alcohol are not food items, and many people who develop cancer don't drink or smoke. Is 'dietary risk' just referring to an inadequate fruit and vegetable intake, or is it referring to other specific foods that we eat? If this is the case, shouldn't these food items be named? Also, how would you square the above death rate from cancer with what the American Cancer Society has stated in their Stewardship Report 2012? Is the statement below at least questionable?

The hopeful side of cancer has never been more hopeful. Most people survive the disease. At the core of this transformation has been the American Cancer Society.

The question is, why has cancer become the number two cause of death in the world? It kills more people annually than those who die as a result of road accidents and wars! As I've already stated, if someone dies as a result of cancer, or in the case of many other diseases, it is described as 'dying from natural causes'. The next question is, how 'natural' it is to die from cancer? Even if dying from cancer was dying from a natural cause, it is conveniently ignored that most people are dying from cancer at *unnatural ages*. According to the Centers for Disease Control and Prevention (CDC): *In the United States, cancer is the second most common cause of death among children between the ages of 1 and 14 years, surpassed only by accidents.* Isn't this incredible? Yet there is not even a national panic. Wow! Shouldn't this qualify as an epidemic? Dr. Tim O'Shea elaborated even further:

Before the 1960s, cancer in children was virtually unheard of. With the skyrocketing number of vaccines and drugs given to children, and the proliferation of snack foods and processed foods in the child diet, by the year 2000 we have the astounding figure of 89.5 deaths per 100,000 population, for all types of cancer combined, below age 19. ([46] CDC website 2010)

Was cancer always a human reality? Well, read what Mike Anderson had to say in his documentary, *The Rave Diet*:

We assume we know more about health and nutrition now than we did back in the eighteen hundreds; yet people living back then did not die because of what they ate. Before the nineteen hundreds, heart disease, our biggest killer, wasn't even included in medical text books. Cancer, diabetes, arthritis, and our other major diseases were rare, and confined to the wealthy, who ate like most Americans eat today...

...meat, dairy products, eggs and fish were uncommon on the plates of working class Americans. It's not that they didn't want these foods; they simply couldn't afford them. But during the 20ᵗʰ century, everything changed. As animal foods become more affordable, Americans

switched from a plant-based diet, to an animal-based diet. This triggered the biggest dietary change in human history, and ushered in a new era of eating related diseases. By the middle of the 20ᵗʰ century, Americans were suddenly dying of heart attacks, and cancer had all the earmarks of an epidemic in the making."

Mike Anderson continues:

...Eating is the biggest cause of disease, disability and death in America today. According to the Surgeon General's report on nutrition and health, "Eating kills two out of three Americans every year". This means, the American eating habit is officially suicidal! ...We have turned eating into the most popular form of unassisted suicide.

If eating kills two out of three people in our western culture, and the number two cause of death is cancer; then food, or what we put in our mouth and call it food, has to be the main cause of cancer. –Author

---

Based on what is known about nutrition and health, it is likely that people did die from what they ate during the eighteen hundreds. This would not be evidenced by statistic because record keeping was not as efficient then as it is now. However, it is very clear in terms of present day statistics that there is an accelerated increase in cancer and other diseases, and that this is due to a shift to a diet and lifestyle that is incompatible with good health.

Do not be misled by the fact that America is the only country mentioned. This applies to all people anywhere who practise a similar diet. Also, do not be misled by the fact that only meat and animal products are mentioned as factors in the proliferation of cancer. Meat and animal based products are by no means the only things that we ingest that cause cancer. This will be apparent when I list and explain later in this book how other foods and drinks cause cancer.

Doctors are expected to be able to explain complicated medical matters to the general public in as simple a language as possible. Have they done so in the case of cancer? Not so that we would notice. Is the subject too complicated for a simple explanation? All information, including that found in the case of cancer research, is not immune to reason and common sense, hence a simple explanation is possible. This is especially true if we have a basic understanding of how our body works. However, even if someone lacks this basic understanding, they should be able to at least grasp the basic logic and common-sense reasoning that surrounds many doctors' opposition to the continued use of chemotherapy drugs to treat cancer. If, at minimum, you come to understand the validity of the reasoning that opposes the use of chemotherapy, this book will be of great value to you. This book is my interpretation of the research and pronouncements of many doctors and other individuals about cancer. It is my interpretation of the answers that research has provided.

Americans are not unique, when people from other parts of the world abandon their traditional plant based diets, and start eating like Americans, they start dying like Americans. – The Rave Diet (DVD documentary)

CHAPTER ONE

THE MYSTERY OF CANCER

If I were to ask you what cancer is, could you explain it to me? Could you give me an explanation as to what happens to the body that makes it becomes cancerous? If the answer is no, the next question is, why not? Isn't it strange that cancer is the number two cause of death in the world, yet most people can't explain it?

Here is another strange phenomenon to consider. Even though heart disease is the number one killer, people are more afraid of cancer. Why is this? People are more afraid of what they don't understand. Cancer is understood to be, at worse, a death sentence and at best, a hit and miss chance of survival. The lack of education about cancer is so severe that for many it is a mystery of mystical proportions. So much so, that many think that cancer can afflict anyone, regardless of their diet or lifestyle. In contrast, heart disease is not regarded in this way because it is not shrouded in mystery. There is not much mystery surrounding heart disease because there is a fair amount of information about what causes it, and how to correct it. Most people understand that the main cause is the existence of blocked arteries. They also understand that if they survive a heart attack it can be remedied with by-pass surgery, or a heart transplant.

Do you find the widespread ignorance about cancer strange, in light of the fact that so much money is invested in cancer research and 'publicity'? The public is constantly being asked to donate towards cancer research, yet I am unaware of any *concerted effort* being made to educate us about the workings of cancer – how to prevent it (apart from stopping smoking), or any other consistent educational information about it. Interestingly, one of the stated objectives of Cancer Research UK is to help them to give people the information they need about cancer. However, how long have they been involved in cancer research and perhaps dispensing this information? For over a hundred years! So they have been dispensing this information for over a hundred years, yet the public is largely ignorant about the workings of this disease. In light of the huge financial resources at their disposal, is this reflected in the size and effectiveness of their publicity?

What information do you suppose people with cancer need? How about how to get rid of it or how to prevent it? What useful information are you aware of regarding cancer before reading this book? If you have useful information, do you think this knowledge is widely known? The question is, what has the combined cancer industry been doing with the extraordinarily large sums of money they receive every day? Have we seen many educational programmes about cancer on prime-time television? Also, in spite of the large sums of money received by cancer researchers, we haven't moved on from the 'no cure' chemotherapy and radiation therapy. These are still the number one treatments of choice. And this has been the case since the 1940s.

So, for nearly seventy years we have a situation where trillions of dollars have been spent, several generations of scientists have invested millions of hours and unquantifiable brain power into finding a solution, yet they have not come up with anything better than drugs that harm the body. Is there not something wrong with this picture?

Imagine applying the above scenario to the Ford motor company. Just imagine Henry Ford being given billions of dollars for development after he made his first Model-T car in 1908. If after seventy years the Model-T is still the best car he'd designed, do you suppose that serious questions would be raised about his integrity? Do you think that, at minimum, questions would be asked about his and the company's competence? The growth of motoring, computing, and various communication technologies are three examples of the natural growth in knowledge of the different challenges that we have taken on. It demonstrates that we generally always advance once we understand the basic fundamentals of a challenge. Since this is a reality of our natural genius, why is there such a vast difference in the progress of the challenge to cure cancer?

What if we compare this lack of progress with other aspects of the medical world, such as surgery? The progress that has been made in surgical knowledge in the past hundred years is staggering. Now we have the reality of keyhole surgery; plastic surgery; heart surgery; kidney transplant; liver transplant; and even bone marrow transplant, to name a few. This is another demonstration that once we understand the basic fundamental of a challenge, we make progress.[2]

---

2 I am aware that some of us do not regard the advancement of surgical knowledge and its various applications as progress. However, in reality, there are circumstances, such as emergencies and when the body reaches a point of no return, where surgery is the *only* option.

Chemotherapy treatment cannot be regarded as progress, especially because it involves the use of drugs that cause extreme damage to the body, and it has been the main approach used, relentlessly, for nearly seventy years!

In the case of cancer research, should we expect that, at minimum, there would be sufficient data and knowledge gathered for the public to be adequately informed? Since the cancer research industry are working on behalf of the public, should we not expect them to use some of the large sums of money they receive to broadcast their findings through the best media possible? In reality, we have a situation where there is still not enough *adequate* information that is *widely available* as to how our cells become cancerous and how to prevent it happening. Why is this so? There are three possible explanations:

- The understanding of cancer is very inadequate, or there are many contradicting views within the industry which leads to there not being a single viewpoint.

- The understanding of how to care for the *health* of the human body is still at a basic level; amongst researchers, therefore, they don't know how to prevent cancer.

- Cancer research has become a business. As such, there is a created inflexibility in approach. This inflexible approach has resulted in the continuous use of a crude and ineffective, but lucrative, *chemical treatment* of the disease. This inflexibility has also resulted in most practitioners being locked in a very blinkered paradigm that does not facilitate finding a solution. If they had been looking in the right direction for over a hundred years they would have come up with definitive answers! The only logical explanation for not discovering a cure is that the medical and pharmaceutical industries have been looking in the wrong direction. This direction doesn't include *natural ways to make the body well*. Therefore, no matter how many trillions of dollars are invested and how much mind-power is invested, or how many millions of hours are invested, an answer will not be found if focus is directed in the wrong direction! This is like walking south in search of the sunrise.

Why I am contending that they have been looking in the wrong direction will become self evident after you consider my research findings on the science of how cancer is developed. I use the word 'developed' deliberately, because my research information suggests that cancer is the result of a process. It is not the result of an event that happens instantly.

Based on what you've read so far, do you think it is reasonable that the cancer industry should be held accountable for the one hundred years plus of failure to eradicate cancer? Should they be held accountable in the same way that any other enterprise would be held accountable if it failed to deliver after so many years of effort and investment? In the case of cancer research, have they been studying cancer cells for over a hundred years without learning how to reverse cancer cell growth without harming the body, or have they been concentrating on finding drugs to kill cancers cells, instead?

The alternative approach suggests learning about the biochemistry of the body; learning about what tilted it out of balance, and therefore learning how to return it to a balanced state. Diseases do not thrive in a body whose biochemistry is in a state of balance. The chemo drugs and radiation approach to treat cancer befits the description of a *scorched-earth policy*. In cancer research, they should be seeking only two answers: how to reverse cancer, and how to prevent it. They should not focus all their energies and resources on finding ways to burn it out of the body! Have you accepted the impression given by the cancer industry that cancer is so complicated and mysterious that it is way beyond our current scientific understanding? Have you accepted that this is the reason why a cure is always 'around the corner' but has still not been found? To accept this as a reality is to also accept that the rise in cancer deaths is unavoidable. Later on, after reading my shared information, you may agree with me that the opposite is true.

It must take an amazing weapon to destroy an amazingly designed body while it is still in its prime. –Author

---

UNDERSTANDING OUR AMAZING BODY

Before I go into my findings about the processes that cause cancer and the actions that the evidence suggests are required to reverse it, let's have a brief look at some of the remarkable characteristics of our bodies. This will serve to underline the awesome intelligence of the body, and illustrate that we have to commit serious crimes against it to circumvent its defences.

Dr. Isaac Jennings stated, *there is no healing force outside the body.* We all know this is true, at least at a basic level. We have all experienced a cut to the skin and observed that the body knows how to congeal the blood, and then create what can be referred to as 'Nature's cast', or a scab. This is a simple, visible demonstration of the body's intelligence. Another basic demonstration of the body's intelligence is the act of vomiting after we have, in our ignorance, loaded our stomach with poisons or incompatible substances. This often occurs after an alcohol binge, or an alcohol and food binge. Vomiting is a survival mechanism. It demonstrates that the body has a built-in intelligence, and its primary drive is to protect and preserve life. It demonstrates that the body can defend itself. It also demonstrates that the body is more intelligent than our minds!

It is important to understand that our entire body is a composite of cells. Our cells require the right biochemistry and this is enabled by an adequate supply of water, oxygen, exercise, sleep, and nutrients to stay healthy, because both health and sickness occur at a cellular level. Therefore, if our cells become cancerous, the reason(s) has/have to be a breakdown in any of the above five supply factors.

Now, let me share some research information that provides the basis for understanding how cells become cancerous. From this research you will see that its findings point to one of the five factors mentioned. If you accept that the five factors mentioned make sense, you should be able to accept the findings of the research. If you accept both the research and the points above, you should have no problem accepting the solution for how to reverse the processes that cause cancer.

Cancer, like many other major life threatening diseases, is a result of our committing major crimes against our body. Every living organism's major drive is the preservation of its life and our body is no different from any other organism in this regard. However, the virtue of our free will can become a vice and unfortunately for the majority of us, we exercise our free will in ways that are not always in our best interest in the preservation of our health and life.

This point cannot be repeated too often: the body is so well designed that it takes a tremendous effort to circumvent all its defence mechanisms and cause it to die prematurely. Another relevant point is this: all living things have a time clock. Elephants generally live for about seventy years, and as I've already mentioned, a fruit fly can only live for a day. It is also well established that human beings can comfortably live up to a hundred years and beyond. So, being disease ridden and dying long before this is un-natural and premature. This is not prevalent in the animal kingdom, except when we interfere with them with our processed foods, chemicals and pollution. We are the only living beings for whom it is common for there to be a very wide disparity in how long we live, within our species. This is outside of being killed intentionally or through accident. Yet we are no less well designed than any other life form. Here are some remarkable facts about our bodies:

- Our heart beats 100,000 times per day.

- We have 60,000 miles of blood vessels; this would wrap around the earth twice at the equator.

- Our blood makes 3,000–5,000 trips per day.

- We have four million skin pores that are constantly changing to keep our body at the appropriate temperature.

- Even with micro chip technology, it would take two buildings the size of the World Trade Centre to match the storage capacity of the brain; and it would take the Hudson River to cool it.

- Our liver, which is our detoxification plant, is made up of cells each of which has 50 different enzymes that do their job a million times per second.

(Source: Anthony Robbins's *Living Health* audio)

This snapshot of our body's remarkable capability should cement the idea of how persistent we have to be in our bad habits to destroy its defences and cause it to die prematurely. It never ceases to amaze me that so many of us accept, without question, that our car would stay in working order if properly serviced, yet find it difficult to accept that the same principle applies to our bodies.

If we understood the amazing construction and workings of our body, we would conclude that it takes an equally amazing effort to destroy it. –Author

---

SO, WHAT IS CANCER?

Cancer is a generic term for a large group of diseases that can affect any part of the body.[3] Other terms used are malignant tumours and neoplasms. One defining feature of cancer is the rapid creation of abnormal cells that grow beyond their usual boundaries, and which can then invade adjoining parts of the body and spread to other organs. This process is referred to as metastasis. Metastases are the major cause of death from cancer. [World Health Organization (WHO) Fact sheet N° 297 (January 2013)].

Naturopaths hold the view that all manifestations of cancer have the same basic underlining cause. Confusion is caused by the promotion of different locations of cancer such as the breast, prostrate, etcetera, as being uniquely different. Confusion is further added to this subject, which is already a mystery to most people, by calling some tumours *benign.* This differentiation into types of tumours does not add clarity to the nature of cancer. This is because, although most benign tumours are not life-threatening, many types of benign tumours have the potential to become cancerous (malignant). So, the public, with the knowledge that there are both malignant and benign tumours, have no greater understanding as to the key question: how do cells become cancerous?

The other confusing term is *remission,* meaning vaguely that the *symptoms* are under control or have disappeared under treatment. Doctors use the word *remission* instead of cure when talking about cancer because they cannot be sure that there are no cancer cells at all in the

---

3 *You will find out later on in this book that there is one area of the body that cancer is very rarely known to affect. This, in itself, will be very revealing about the nature of cancer.*

body. So the cancer could come back in the future, although there is no sign of it at the time.

This is clearly a non-scientific term, since it cannot be either measured or quantified. Many people die after been told that their cancer was in 'remission'. This included my aunt, who was also given the all-clear before the cancer 'came back' and killed her. In reality, either you have a disease, or you don't have the disease. How many have died because of this incompetence within the cancer industry? What then is the cause for *the rapid creation of abnormal cells* that we call cancer?

THE EXPERIMENTS THAT INDICATED THE CURE

DR. WARBURG'S EXPERIMENT

Dr. Otto Heinrich Warburg (October 8, 1883 – August 1, 1970) was a German physiologist, medical doctor and one of the 20th century's leading *biochemists*. In 1931 he won the Nobel Prize in Physiology or Medicine for his research in cellular respiration.

In 1924, Dr. Warburg hypothesized that *cancer*, malignant growth, and *tumour* growth are caused by tumour cells mainly generating *energy* by *non-oxidative breakdown of glucose*.[4] Dr. Warburg spent a great deal of time studying the life of our cells, specialising in cellular respiration. He hypothesised that since life and death happens at the cellular level, the most important element is oxygen. So he asked the question: if something was cutting off oxygen supply, would it cause the cells to not only die, but to mutate? Mutated cells are said to be cancer cells. Mutated cells are cells that have been damaged, and one of the characteristics of mutated cells is the reduction in their ability to adequately utilise oxygen.

In his bid to find answers as to whether cells would die or mutate if deprived of oxygen, he took cells from rats and put them in bell jars. One jar was fully oxygenated, as would be the case in the rat's body. In the other jar, he reduced the oxygen by about 80%. In this latter jar all of the cells died. The same thing occurred at a 75% reduction of oxygen. At a 60% reduction of oxygen, all of the cells weakened; some died, but the majority of them mutated. Here we can see that the link between insufficient oxygen and disease was firmly established and it has been so for a very long time.

4 In a healthy state, the body breaks-down glucose for energy by utilising oxygen (oxidation)

It has also been established that once the level of oxygen available to a cell drops below 60% of normal supply, the cell is forced to switch to an inferior method of energy production – fermentation. This process produces lactic acid and a lot more carbon dioxide than the healthy method of energy production, which is the oxidation of glucose/sugar. So, the now mutated cells are in an environment that is more acidic because of fermentation, and where there is more carbon dioxide than oxygen. Since the body's number one drive is to maintain life, the cells utilize what is mostly available in its attempt to survive. It utilizes carbon dioxide. This is part of the basic process of the cells proliferating or reproducing themselves rapidly.

Cancer occurs where mutated cells are stuck in the mode of reproducing themselves by utilising carbon dioxide instead of oxygen. The reproduction of cancer cells is called *metastasis*. Metastasis is the spreading of cancer. If this process is not halted, the person will eventually die. The body cannot survive with too many cells that are mainly 'living' off carbon dioxide instead of oxygen. A fully oxygenated body does not die from cancer.

When the tissues and organs are overloaded by acidity the transport of oxygen is strangled. This suffocation means the cells cannot breathe properly. Every cell in our body needs to breathe new oxygen and to clear acidic carbon dioxide to function correctly. – Marcus Julian Felicetti (naturopath & yoga therapist), September 24th 2012

(http://www.mindbodygreen.com/0-6243/How-to-Balance-Your-pH-to-Heal-Your-Body.html)

Understanding that in a state of cancer the cells in the body switch to an inferior method of producing energy, which is called fermentation, is important. It is why people die from cancer. In a healthy state, the body produces its energy from glucose-oxidation. *Glucose*-oxidation is a chemical process that provides energy [through the molecular product known as Adenosine Tri-Phosphate (ATP)] for the body to carry out all of its required activities. If the body is producing less and less energy, or less and less ATP, it weakens to the point where it cannot carry out its required functions. So cells die; tissues die; organs die, and eventually the person dies.

Even more conducive to cancer is a setting of fermentation. That means half-digested carbohydrates. Every bootlegger knows that as sugars ferment, they bubble. The bubbles are the oxygen leaving. Cancer doesn't like oxygen too well, but it loves sugar. Starting to get the picture here? Fermentation means half-digested, oxygen-poor. This oxygen-deprived environment is perfect for cancer – it thrives in it. Fermentation creates an acidic environment and keeps oxygen away. – Dr. Tim O'Shea (www. thedoctorwithin.com)

Dr. Harry Goldblatt also published a study on the relationship between oxygen and malignant cells in the Journal of Experimental Medicine (1953). He did the same experiment as Dr. Warburg and obtained the same result. However, he decided to take it a little bit further. He took cells that were fully oxygenated and put them in rats; and he took cells that had mutated because of insufficient oxygen and injected them into other rats. The rats that had been injected with the fully oxygenated cells did not develop cancer. Every one of the rats that were injected with the mutated cells developed cancer. This proves even further that mutated cells are cancer cells and their character is to proliferate.

*Cancer, above all other diseases, has countless secondary causes. But, even for cancer, there is only one prime cause. Summarized in a few words, **the prime cause of cancer** is the replacement of the respiration of oxygen in normal body cells by a fermentation of sugar.* – Dr. Otto H. Warburg in a Lecture.

Based on what you've read so far, it has to be an inescapable conclusion that to deprive cells of oxygen creates a critical cause for the development of cancer. So how did some doctors respond to this information? According to Wikipedia:

The concept that cancer cells switch to fermentation in lieu of aerobic respiration has become widely accepted, **even if it is not seen as the cause of cancer.** *Some suggest the Warburg phenomenon could be used to develop anticancer drugs.* [Emphasis mine]

They were right *if* they were suggesting that the switching of cancer cells to fermentation/*anaerobic respiration* instead of using oxygen to survive is not the root cause of cancer. I don't *think* this is what they were suggesting. They totally downgraded the role oxygen deprivation plays in the cause of cancer. If they were thinking about *root causes,* they would have concluded that the root cause of cancer would be *whatever causes cells to lose their oxygen supply in the first place.* They would have focused on what caused the cell to switch its mode of survival from the oxygenation of glucose, to surviving on the fermentation of glucose. The focus should have been on the fact that the reduction of oxygen to the cell (lost of oxidative breakdown) is the catalyst for the cell to mutate and become cancerous.

Fermentation is a process that does not require oxygen. Warburg is saying that cells switch to the fermentation of glucose to survive and that fermentation also produces carbon dioxide. The cells are therefore now using carbon dioxide to survive, as they are only getting a little oxygen. This means the cells are now behaving like a plant in terms of 'breathing in/absorbing' carbon dioxide. If the cells get stuck into this mode of using carbon dioxide to survive, we now have mutated cells that multiply rapidly, or proliferate, and this is what is called cancer.

THE ACIDIC FACTOR OF THE WARBURG EXPERIMENT

Mutated cells will proliferate as long as the state of the body's biochemistry, at the time when cancer growth was triggered, remains the same. Warburg reported that cancer cells maintained a lower pH balance (i.e. more acidic): as low as 6.0, due to lactic acid production and the increase of CO_2 (carbon dioxide). This suggests that cancer thrives in an acidic state or medium. If enough lactic acid is generated by cancer cells, then the body is reduced to a dangerous acidic state (a low pH). A pH measure is a measurement of the body's acidity. It is, therefore, a measurement of the body's wellbeing. The total pH scale ranges from 1 to 14, with 7 considered to be neutral. A pH less than 7 is said to be acidic, and solutions with a pH greater than 7 are alkaline. Our ideal pH balance is slightly alkaline – around 7.30 to 7.45. A pH balance of 6, as Dr. Warburg reported, is an unhealthy acidic state. The pH balance of the body is very important to sustain good health and life. The pH chart below indicates that there is a point of acidity within our blood at which we cannot survive. It is primarily diet and lifestyle that can transform a healthy alkaline blood/body to such a deadly acidic state. Marcus Julian Felicetti, a naturopath and yoga therapist wrote:

Some health experts believe that our pH balance is extremely important, others say it is essential, there are a few who clearly state that it is a matter of life and death. The only people who don't emphasize the alkaline/acidity balance as central to health are quacks that peddle a pharmaceutical pill for every ill, a drug for every bug.

(http://www.mindbodygreen.com/0-6243/How-to-Balance-Your-pH-to-Heal-Your-Body.html)

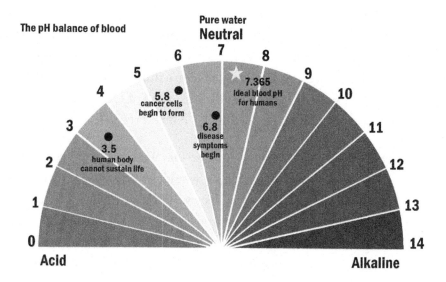

According to the book, *Reverse Aging*, by Sang T. Whang: "Blood that is pH 7.3 actually has 69.4% less oxygen than blood with pH 7.45". If this is true, tackling the acidity of the body is paramount in the fight against cancer. If such a small difference in pH, within the healthy alkaline range, has such a drastic effect on the flow of oxygen, then a highly acidic blood, which is known to have a great restriction on the level of oxygen flow in the blood, would play a big part in the process that causes cancer. This is in line with the findings of Dr. Warburg. It is important to understand that a highly acidic blood is caused by a highly acidic diet and lifestyle.

In a state of cancer the body would be highly acidic because fermentation produces excess lactic acid, alcohol and carbon dioxide. It seems that it would be a good idea to counter this by alkalising the body with alkalising foods. – Author

---

By stating that Dr. Warburg's evidence does not explain the cause of cancer, the doctors, as earlier mentioned, must have meant that they did not understand why the cells start duplicating themselves once they had mutated. Otherwise, it would be tantamount to saying, "A person was run over by a car but we don't think that is what caused their death." I can't imagine them dismissing all of Dr. Warburg's findings, because his findings earned him a Nobel Prize.

If those doctors had chosen to look at Dr. Warburg findings from a simple cause and effect approach, it would have led them to a food and herb solution. This is because they would have first sought to find out what causes cells to lose their oxygen supply. This would have led them to the discovery of the effect that animal products, processed foods, alcohol, and other substances have on the body's cells in terms of the restriction of their uptake of oxygen, and their ability to utilise oxygen. Secondly, they would have sought to find ways to return the normal oxygen flow to the cells; and this would have led them to the first, obvious factor: the elimination of all foods and substances that create an unhealthy, over-acidic blood/body and cause cells to suffer from an oxygen-starvation crisis. Thirdly, they would have looked to herbs that are known to take oxygen to our cells. Fourthly, they would have sought to find ways to strengthen the immune system; and this would have led them to fruits, vegetables, herbs, vitamins and minerals. However, this was not the paradigm they were working in; they were looking for a drugs solution – and they still are. Perhaps, what restricted their approach more was that they were, and are, looking for a *patentable-drug* solution.

Synopsis

The following is how I break down the above information for my own clarity:

- In the healthy action of our body, oxygen plus glucose/sugar (oxidation) equals energy.

- In the healthy action of our body, oxygen plus glucose/sugar (oxidation) also produces carbon dioxide.

- A healthy body does not use the carbon dioxide because it is a poison; and too much carbon dioxide in our body will kill us. Carbon dioxide (CO_2) is what we breathe out and what plants absorb.

- In a cancerous state, cells lose their ability to fully utilise oxygen to create energy.

- In a cancerous state, the cells resort to a poor method of producing energy which is fermentation of glucose/sugar. This is where the glucose is turned into lactic acid, alcohol, and carbon dioxide.

- Fermentation is a method of cells respiration/breathing without oxygen (anaerobic).

- If a person with cancer continues with a high acidic diet, such as is the case with animal based foods, this would be a lethal combination, because cancer strives in an acidic medium/body.

- General good health dictates that the body should be more alkaline than acidic.

- If the effects of fermentation are not countered, the cancer victim's body would have too much acid, alcohol, and far too much carbon dioxide for it to sustain life. The excessive lactic acid, alcohol and carbon dioxide are a result of the cancer cells using the carbon dioxide within the body to grow. These cells will then disrupt normal body functions, and once this happens, the organs that contain them literally start to shut down.

- The human body cannot survive with an over acidic pH balance.

- **Healthy pancreas**

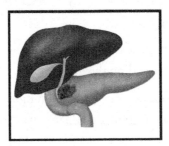

- Healthy cells thrive in an environment that is mostly alkaline.

- **Cancerous pancreas**

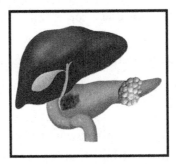

- Cells damaged by alcohol, drugs, junk foods, etc., or as a result of oxygen starvation due to clogged veins and arteries caused by ingesting animal cholesterol, refined carbohydrates, processed sugars, and other foreign substances such as tobacco smoke with its tar, cyanide, formaldehyde, methanol (wood alcohol), acetylene and ammonia, will suffer a reduction in their ability to carry or utilise oxygen.

- Due to a reduction of oxygen, cells mutate (change their form or their nature). **This is part one of the cancer process.**

* To survive, cells combine carbon dioxide and glucose (fermentation) for energy. **This is part two of the cancer process.**

* Cancer cells multiply (metastasise/spread). **This is part three of the cancer process.**

* *Now life is threatened.*

* Cancer cells thrive in acidic environment.

Since all the evidence points to us being vegetarians or fruitarians, and since vegetables and fruits are mainly alkaline forming, then our body's health is better maintained through their consumption. The proof that we are herbivores (vegetarians or fruitarians) will be illustrated later in this book. Those who practise naturopathic medicine suggest that our diet should be at least 70% alkaline and 30% acidic. The acidic part of our diet does not have to come from animal based products. Some plant based foods are acidic, such as nuts. A switch to a culture of predominantly eating animal based products would make most people's body have a high acidic pH balance. In such an acidic state, the body is more susceptible to diseases, including cancer.

I have found that addressing an over acidic system is fundamental to bringing the body back to vitality. – Marcus Julian Felicetti (naturopath & yoga therapist)

The quality of our lives is the quality of our cells. – *Anthony Robbins*

CHAPTER TWO

Oxygen is king

The following points are known facts about the relationship between oxygen deprivation and two other major illnesses.

- If the brain is deprived of oxygen, one can get a stroke.
- If the heart is deprived of oxygen, one gets a heart attack.

It is also a known scientific fact that if the tissues and cells of the body are deprived of oxygen, this presents the underlying cause of all cancers. Unfortunately, though, this fact thus far has not resulted in it being the basis for the reversal of the disease.

When we weigh up all that we know about the human body, it is an inescapable truth that our priorities of nutrition should be as follows:

- Uninterrupted infusion of unpolluted oxygen to our cells as the number one most important element of good health;
- Next is clean, unpolluted water;

- Thirdly are vitamins, minerals and enzymes (preferably those found in fruits and vegetables); and

- Fourthly, carbohydrates and proteins.

The following nutrients – water, vitamins, minerals, carbohydrates, and proteins are not easily separated from each other. This is so because they are often found combined in fruits, vegetables and nuts. As a result, they could all be listed as the second nutritional priority. It would be instructional for many to look at the nutritional information on a box of orange juice and notice that carbohydrate and protein are listed as ingredients. In spite of the importance of vitamins, minerals, and enzymes in maintaining health, most people embrace a diet overburdened by carbohydrates and proteins, and the majority of those that are eaten are of an unhealthy nature.

Incidentally, this understanding about the importance of oxygen removes the oddity from a desire to sleep in an oxygen chamber. The importance of oxygen should also not be misinterpreted as suggesting exercises will prevent cancer. The body requires a totally healthy lifestyle in order to protect it from premature illness. Many people have a lifestyle of 'add and subtract'. They give the body the benefits of exercise, and then minimise the benefits by clogging up their arteries with animal (unhealthy) cholesterol, killing their cells with alcohol, and starving their bodies with denatured and processed foods.

Aerobic type of exercises on their own will not prevent cancer because the process that causes cancer also involves the change of the body's biochemistry from more alkaline to more acidic. An acidic type of diet, high in cholesterol, food chemicals, and other chemicals, plus a toxic lifestyle is the main causes of cancer. Once the cancer process starts, it produces even more acids, and this exacerbates the unhealthy and dangerous acidic imbalance within the body. So, unless the acidic imbalance and other factors, such as excessive stress, that restrict the flow of oxygen are reversed, exercise on its own will not be enough to prevent cancer. This is why many get cancer even though they exercise regularly.

Because we have been mis-educated for so long about the real causes of diseases, the role that oxygen deprivation plays in ill health and major diseases cannot be emphasised enough. Our body is our most important asset. If we misuse it, we have nowhere else to live. Its correct care is one aspect of our human experience that we cannot afford to misunderstand or to miscalculate. We cannot afford this misunderstanding because, if we do, the bad habits may reduce the body to a state of no return.

As this subject is one of life and death, I feel the necessity to be blunt. If we misunderstand how to care for our body, or how to overcome cancer, should we find ourselves with this disease, it would lead to either premature death, or survival in such a poor state of health that such a life may feel as if it's not worth living. The discomfort of poor health can be of such magnitude that if the person does not wish for death, their suffering may have to be endured for decades.

If this is the first time you've been made aware that we have been deceived about health and cancer, please research everything that I've said in this book. Of course, your approach will depend upon whether or not you accept that current cancer treatment is deeply flawed.

If you are still not convinced that oxygen is the king of good health, consider these three questions:

- How long can we survive without food? We can survive 7-8 weeks without food, depending on body weight, temperature and exertion.

- How long can we survive without water? We can survive between 8-14 days without water, depending on how fast the body loses fluid.

- How long can we survive without oxygen? Brain cells die within 4 to 6 minutes. When the flow of oxygen to the brain is completely cut off, a person will lose consciousness within 10 seconds. Extended hypoxia (oxygen deprivation) leads to brain damage and ultimately, to death.

Cells die = tissues die = organ dies = you die

To repeat an important point, both health and sickness occur at the cellular level. The following experiment demonstrates that synthetic drugs have no place in the care and health of our cells. It shows that in a controlled environment, our cells could live beyond their 'normal' time span if given adequate oxygen, water and nutrients:

Dr. Alexis Carrel (June 28, 1873 – November 5, 1944) was a French surgeon and biologist who was awarded the Nobel Prize in Physiology or Medicine in 1912 for pioneering vascular suturing techniques. He invented the first perfusion pump with Charles A. Lindbergh; opening the way for organ transplantation. While at the Rockefeller Institute for Medical Research, he kept samples of heart tissue from a chicken embryo alive for 29 years. Immersed in a solution from which they obtained all the necessary nutrients, the embryo cells excreted their metabolic wastes into the same solution. Each day, the old solution was discarded and replaced with fresh broth. After living for 29 years, the chicken heart tissue died when the assistant forgot to change the polluted fluid.

Dr. Carrel comments: *The cell is immortal. It is merely the fluid in which it floats that degenerates. Renew this fluid at regular intervals [detoxification]; give the cell something on which to feed [proper diet & nutrition] and as far as we know, the pulsation of life may go on forever.* [Author's comments inserted].

Part of this nutrition would clearly include oxygen, since healthy cells cannot remain healthy without oxygen. As we all have been made aware, oxygen is the nutrient that cells can survive without for the shortest length of time. Dr. Carrel's experiment is a powerful testimonial of how vital it is for the body to maintain its ability to detoxify itself. If it were practical to live in a manner that would facilitate our cells being kept in a constant state of nourishment, as in Dr. Carrel's experiment, we could, at minimum, live a very long and healthy life. It is clear that a clean environment for our cells facilitates good health and long life. Therefore, *any synthetic drug added to this environment will interfere with the body's ability to detoxify itself, and therefore weaken the body.*

When our lifestyle and/or diet kills or weakens our cells beyond the ideal, it also reduces the body's ability to utilise oxygen. The process of the body utilising oxygen and nutrients is what gives the body its energy. This energy plays a vital role in the detoxification process. Ultimately, a lack of energy results in death. Here is another case that corresponds to the principle of Dr. Carrel's experiment. It demonstrates the power of keeping our body in the right balance:

Bob Davis claimed to have healed his prostate cancer by colon cleansing/detoxification, diet, juice fasting, as well as determination! He stated:

Does cleansing work? In June 2001, I was diagnosed with severe prostate cancer and I was immediately pressed to have surgery. Instead I went on a cleansing program and three weeks later my doctor said, 'I don't know what you are doing but keep it up. You have no prostate cancer'.
(http://www.healingcancernaturally.com/detoxification.html)

Everything that goes into the body has to be either assimilated or eliminated – Anthony Robbins

Dr. Albert Wahl said, *"Disease is due to a deficiency in the oxidation process of the body, leading to an accumulation of toxin".* As already stated, the oxidation process, which involves a combination of oxygen and glucose/sugar, is what gives the body energy to carry out its vital functions. Cleansing the body of toxins is one such vital function. The liver and kidneys are two of the main organs that cleanse the body of toxins. If they are weakened by a reduction of energy production, we become prone to diseases, including cancer.

Dr. Wendell Hendricks of the Hendricks Research Foundation wrote, *"Cancer is a condition within the body where the oxidation has become so depleted that the body cells have degenerated beyond control. The body is so overloaded with toxins that it sets up a tumour mass to harbour these poisons and remove them from general activity within the body."*

He is suggesting that a malignant tumour is a creation of the body's intelligence, and it is done because of the body's drive to protect its life. It does this by removing the cancer cells from general circulation within the body, so that they do not become widespread. So, in effect, the dreaded 'lump' is the intelligent body's way of 'corralling' the cancer cells. The malignant tumour is therefore like a cocoon filled with cancer cells.

The evidence from these doctors' research is conclusive: oxygen plays the primary role in health and well-being. I am going to pose a question that should cement the understanding that oxygen deprivation is the key factor that causes cancer. However, before I pose this question, let's have look at the most common or popular locations for cancer:

Bladder
Breast
Cervix
Colon
Endometrium
Oesophagus
Gall-bladder
Kidney
Liver
Mouth
Ovaries
Pancreas
Pharynx
Prostate
Rectum
Stomach
Testicles
Thyroid
Uterus
Vulva
Skin
Brain

These are by no means the only locations for cancer. Cancer *doesn't seem* to have any respect for any part of the body. So, the question is this, why is it that people very rarely die of cancer of the heart? Have you ever heard of this happening? I certainly haven't. People very rarely get cancer of the heart because that's where the most highly oxygenated blood is, and cancer doesn't like oxygen! Cancer likes an anaerobic environment. The more anaerobic the environment, the more favourable it is to cancer growth. The fact that the heart is constantly pumping blood, and oxygen, seem to have made it almost immune to cancer. According to the Mayo Clinic:

Heart cancer is extremely rare. For example, a review of more than 12,000 autopsies identified only seven cases of primary cardiac tumor — an incidence of less than 0.1 percent. At Mayo Clinic, on average only one case of heart cancer is seen each year. Although still rare, most cancers found in the heart have come from elsewhere in the body. These include lymphomas that originate in the chest near the heart. Other cancers that can spread to the heart include melanomas and sarcomas.

In addition to seeing an average of one case of heart cancer per year, the article also stated, *The vast majority of heart tumors are noncancerous (benign).*

(http://www.mayoclinic.com/health/heart-cancer/AN01288)

WHAT SHOULD HAVE BEEN THE LOGICAL CONCLUSION AND ACTIONS FROM DR. OTTO WARBURG'S EXPERIMENT?

Let's take another look at what was said about Dr. Warburg's findings, and see if it provides a clue as to why we are in the position that we are in today:

The concept that cancer cells switch to fermentation in lieu of aerobic respiration has become widely accepted, even if it is not seen as the cause of cancer. Some suggest the Warburg phenomenon could be used to develop anticancer drugs.

Many have accepted that cells switch from the healthy (alkaline) use of oxygen, plus glucose/sugar (oxidation) to produce energy, to a process of the unhealthy acidic fermentation of glucose/sugars, to produce an inferior type of energy, and that this leads to cancer. Yet some scientists' response to this switch to an acidic, and non-oxygenated environment, was to suggest that a drug should be developed to fix this problem. Fermentation creates an acidic environment; therefore, this should guide and inform the initial, logical approach to correct or cure the disease, which is to reverse the environment surrounding the cells to a more alkaline one. Shouldn't the objective be to return the cells to using oxygen to produce energy, and thus let the cancer cells die a natural death because they don't thrive in an oxygenated and alkaline environment?

I find it impossible to comprehend why they did not conclude that oxygen deprivation was the primary cause of cancer. A wild guess would be that they were locked into the germ-theory paradigm. This is a belief system that claims that all diseases are caused by germs. However, there is one thing that we can conclude for sure; they were locked in a drugs cure paradigm. The fact that we are currently locked into a massive drugs-suppressant medical system is testament that they were locked into this paradigm.

The germ theory is a narrow view that has been adopted by the current medical establishment, which conveniently relies on a profitable cut, burn, and poison approach to sickness. – Marcus Julian Felicetti (naturopath & yoga therapist)

Even though Dr. Warburg discovered that oxygen deprivation caused cells to mutate, there was no mention as to what causes cells to be deprived of oxygen. Cancer was not shown to be related to diet. However, this could have been a simple conclusion to flow from his discovery. The general lack of knowledge of the link between foods and cancer has helped to foster the dominant culture of unhealthy eating and the junk food industry. The phenomenal growth of the junk food industry has resulted in an explosion of diseases and ill health, and this has, in turn, fuelled the growth of the pharmaceutical drugs industry.

In the development of any culture, it is comparatively easy for any group to take the forefront in terms of the type of medicine that is practiced. This is because, unlike other deep beliefs that we have, medicine does not evoke deep emotional divisions among us. Unfortunately for us, the system that took the forefront was the pharmaceutical industry. This industry was founded on a drugs-to-cure disease principle and it produces what is known as allopathic medicine.

It has grown into a multi-trillion dollar industry, and its main characteristic is that it suppresses symptoms of diseases. It does not *cure* any of the major diseases. If you have any of the major diseases, you will never go to any doctor and be told that this or that medicine will cure you after 'x' number of days, weeks, months or years. Even the common cold is said to have no cure. It is therefore no secret that the entire, allopathic, medical system is primarily a 'no cure' industry. Yet, amazingly, very few people find this strange enough to question it.

This is a major example of how easy it is for people to accept any reality as normal. This acceptance of drug suppressant treatments as 'normal' is so dangerous, yet hundreds of millions of people accept the reality of taking pharmaceutical drugs for a *lifetime*!

Diseases are a result of doing incompatible things to the body that throws its biochemistry out of balance. Even though allopathic medicine suppresses symptoms, no other approach can be successful without the person ceasing to do incompatible things to their body. This is to say, healing is not a single event. The other major objection to the allopathic approach is the common array of side-effects/damages that it does to the body and a person's health. What I am advocating is a non-harmful approach to medicine and healing.

Surgery, radiation, and pharmaceutical drugs are invasive approaches that are ineffective because they work against the body's natural function to heal itself and it fails to address the underlying cause and only treats the symptoms. – Marcus Julian Felicetti (naturopath & yoga therapist)

Is it that we are so dumb that we cannot find cures for the major diseases, even after researching for, at least, over a century? I don't think so. The answer is that the current medical system is locked in a paradigm that says only drugs can treat diseases. So, after more than a century, should we conclude that the human body is not receptive to drugs? If we do, should we also conclude that there can be no cures for the major diseases if we continue in this paradigm?

After what I have illustrated with Dr. Warburg's experiment, you should find it strange that we are still having a situation where cancer is growing at an alarming rate. The basic laws of life and the universe are that everything has a cause and effect process. Therefore, you should refuse to accept that, after years of constant research, with billions or trillions of dollars spent, we are still not capable of explaining the rudiments of cancer and how to prevent it.

A more accurate explanation for the prevalence of ignorance among the majority is rooted in the following question: whose job is it to educate us to the point of our being capable of preventing ourselves from developing cancer? The simple answer would be the cancer research and treatment industry. If they did this job very well, might it not result in at least a diminishing of the industry, or ultimately the disappearance of the industry? Can you see a conflict of interest in this position? Is it serving them better to concentrate on treating the damage instead of preventing it, therefore guaranteeing that they keep their jobs?

As you will become aware, some of the causes of cancer are well known within the medical and science community. How many of these causes are widely known to the public? So, why aren't they using their enormous resources to educate the public, and to campaign against these causes of cancer? Does this situation not prove that it is, at best, not their focus, and at worse, it is not in their self-interest to do so? The fact that they spend the majority of their resources on research and developing cancer drugs demonstrates their primary focus.

Since significant research agencies have started, the estimated total donated into cancer research sits at $4 Trillion – (wiki.answers.com)

We should find it astonishing that this much money has been spent without finding a cure; and even more curious is the fact that there is a constant request for donations for research purposes. As I've already noted, one of the stated objectives of Cancer Research UK is to, "help them give people the information they need about cancer." I would expect that all the other research agencies around the world would have something like this as an objective. Yet, in spite of the extraordinarily large funding that these organisations receive, we never see a measure of broadcasted information/education that reflects the large sums of money they receive. Should we assume that the money mainly goes towards large wages and profits? If most of it goes into research, how comes we haven't moved from the destructive chemotherapy drugs and radiation situation, even after a hundred years?

The only way that, after investing so much time and resources into finding a cure, we are no closer to a cure and it is still a mystery to the public at large, would be because they have been looking in the wrong direction. Alternatively it is because their self-interest is so great that they are not motivated to find a cure. What do you think?

Understanding the possible reasons why the system has been stuck into this suppressant-drug paradigm is very important. We also need to understand why the system has lasted this long, with no cure in sight.

IS THERE A CONSPIRACY?

The alternative to thinking that the cancer industry has not solved the cancer problem because they have been looking in the wrong direction is too shocking to consider – this being that they have the information, but have deliberately kept the public ignorant. Some think this is the case. I do not. I think it is a lot more complicated than this. Though there is evidence that they are actively clamping down on natural remedies, there is no simple conspiracy where everyone and every organisation within this lucrative industry get together in a smoky room. It is more a case of them instinctively protecting their market share.

I think that those who initiated the system did so with good intentions. However, because they started off with a "germs-cause-diseases" theory and a "drugs-cure- diseases" theory, this mushroomed, and inertia eventually kicked in. Once inertia had kicked in, it eventually became global. This inevitably created many layers of self-interest and systems within systems that are fixed in place like cement. The overall system has no scope, or impetus, for self examination. Such self examination would lead to the inevitable conclusion that they need to at least modify, and at most, completely dismantle, what they are doing. If there is a 'conspiracy', it would be more in the form of turning a blind eye, motivated by self-interest. However, you can draw your own conclusions by examining the following information written by Dr. Tim O'Shea:

The American Cancer Society, *for example, collects hundreds of millions per year. Very little of this money ever finds its way to research. The majority of the money goes into investments and towards administration – lavish salaries and perqs for the Society's officers and employees. A funny thing is that written into the charter of the American Cancer Society is the clause that states that if a cure for cancer is ever found, on that day, the Society will disband. So is this an organization that is going to be motivated to find a cure for cancer?*

*Throughout the 1980s, working through Nixon's illusory War on Cancer, we were spending less than $50 billion per year on cancer. By 2009 the total spent on cancer care, treatment and research exceeded **$305 billion** per year, according to the* British *Medical Journal, 28 August 2009.*

– Dr. Tim O'Shea

This system has mastered the art of doing the wrong thing very well. It has grown so large that it has become proficient at stifling every alternative treatment and potential cure that is natural and compatible with the human body. Allopathic medicine is so dominant and has so much control, you might belief that we are not living in the spirit of western democracy.

The allopathic medical system has never made it a secret that they have no cures for the major diseases, including cancer. This tells us that if we are looking for a cure right now, we should look elsewhere. Yet, alternative cures are not encouraged. In the case of cancer, chemotherapy drugs and radiation have no track record of curing the disease. If they did, the expression, "Go to the hospital to get cured," would be commonplace. However, these treatments are fully backed by the authorities that control the medical system. In contrast, take a look at the list of 'unproven methods' that they are up against according to Dr. Tim O'Shea:

The American Cancer Society and the FDA have a list of "Unproven Methods" for cancer, which they attack with their full measure of invective, both directly and using their many covers. As you might expect, the criteria for getting on this list are predictable:

- *a natural form*
- *non-toxic*
- *not produced by the Drug Industry*
- *easily available without a prescription*
- *inexpensive*
- *non-patentable*

He goes on to say: *Even though chemotherapy and radiation and palladium implants are completely unproven themselves, and frequently are the cause of death themselves, they are not on the Unproven List. Why not? Because they're expensive, can be completely controlled, and are patentable.*

According to an article by *News Target*, which was published on July 31, 2005: *Most of the treatments on the "Unproven Methods" list have never been shown to be ineffective or dangerous. More than 100 promising therapies have been discredited by the American Cancer Society in this way. One such therapy was the Gerson therapy.* The article also stated: *Many board members, in fact, stand to make much more money from treating cancer than from preventing it. It has also been argued that their ties to polluting industries has led the industry to wilfully suppress information about the environmental causes of cancer… several American Cancer Society board members are CEOs or presidents of biotechnology companies. (http://www.facts-are-facts.com/news/sne-71206-cancersociety.ihtml)*

Biotechnology companies are involved in pharmaceutical therapies and diagnostic tests. Can the above be construed as an inherent conflict of interest?

Those who have power within the cancer industry have been banning or restricting many non-patentable herbal remedies for years. The question is, why? The problem in the cancer industry is this: there is far more money to be made from treating diseases than from curing or preventing them, and this fact has thus created conflicts of interest. As I've stated, I don't *think* the industry started out with this as their intention. This surgical and suppressant medicine industry just naturally evolved into what it is today, because the people who eventually took centre stage were looking in the wrong direction at the beginning. The principle of inertia took effect like a snowball rolling down a hill. Once this system took root and became super-lucrative, the natural human inclination of self-interest became embedded.

The self-interest that keeps this ineffective medical system in place is complicated and has various tenets to it. One of the consequences of the inertia that snow-balled this type of medicine into the giant that it has become is that this type of medicine has become embedded within western culture.

Through various processes, including television programmes such as 'ER' (Emergency Room), allopathic approaches to medicine have been glamorised and elevated to a highly respected status. The ordinary public, who were not educated about natural remedies and who have been discouraged from seeking them, are the same people who become doctors and medical drug researchers. Since illness can be life threatening and because the public is generally ignorant about looking after themselves, doctors often take on a Godlike status, especially if we find ourselves in a life or death situation.

Our socialisation into believing in allopathic medicine and the status that we bestow on doctors, are the reasons why so many of us are stuck into accepting this type of medicine as the first port of call when we are ill. We are stuck like this because the situation is similar to the reason we tend to accept a certain point of view. We tend to accept the dominant belief and activity of whatever culture matrix we find ourselves. This is just as true of medicine as it is of sport and many other traditions.

So why are the administrators stuck in their current suppressant mode of treatment? They are stuck there because they have inherited and expanded a super-large, multi-trillion dollar industry that has layers upon layers of job creation and the possibilities of creating more jobs. The cancer industry facilitates the provision of prestigious positions such as chief researchers, consultants and doctors and this creates an inflexible socio economic self-interest structure. The people at the top of this extremely lucrative business structure are not motivated to change or dismantle the source of their wealth and lifestyle. Their self-interest is primarily of an economic nature.

Those who are socialised to revere this system, to such an extent that they become doctors, would have the self-interest of having a highly paid job, a desire to maintain their prestigious position and recognition, as well as a desire to help people using the medicine that they believe in. As a result of all of this, they are likely to be both suspicious and even hostile towards what they call alternative medicine. This is primarily because of their training and the stigma our culture attaches to alternative remedies.

Doctors are not 'bad people'. Like most of us, they are not inclined to embrace what they don't know. You would have thought that, because they work in a system that has no cure for the major diseases, they should be genuinely interested in curing people and so be eager to investigate an alternative solution. However, the job description of doctors, such as general practitioners, does not include looking for cures. They are expected only to *practise* what they were taught! They dispense whatever medicine is approved and wait for new developments from those in research. Those in research are looking for solutions within the confines of chemicals that can suppress or burn away diseased cells. They are in the business of suppressing symptoms of diseases. They are not in the business of curing the underlying causes of diseases. These causes cannot be fixed with drugs. Doctors' roles in all of this are quite understandable, because one would not normally go against years of training and embrace what is neither known, nor believed in.

From this you should realise that pharmacists and doctors, such as general practitioners and surgeons, are not the ones who are at the forefront of deciding the direction of the allopathic medical system. They all rely on the pharmaceutical companies for their direction.

Even if they were, it would probably not make much difference because of another major flaw in how they are trained.

The first flaw I've already mentioned: they are trained to believe in a medicine that suppresses the symptoms of diseases, rather than curing or preventing them. The next flaw is that they primarily study pathology. This means they primarily study the causes, the nature and effects of *diseases* within the narrow confines of either a germ/virus, bad gene (inherited), or bad cells – hence, cancer cells are bad/rogue cells that have to be destroyed. This is why they study dead bodies. A naturopath has no interest in dead bodies.

According to life coach Anthony Robbins: *As a result of the allopathic approach, approximately 4000 people die each day from cancer and heart disease in America; yet, one in every ten dollars spent in America is spent on health care. Wouldn't this suggest that this approach is not working?*

The opposite of studying diseases is to study wellness. A disease is the *symptom* of the problem, and can only be solved by eliminating the cause. A great analogy that depicts the studying of disease approach, as told by Anthony Robbins is the story of a man who was by a lake. He heard a loud splash, and saw two people drowning. He rescued them, but before he could recover from his exertions, the same thing happened, and there were four more who needed rescuing. This continued until he was unable to save anymore people. However, this disaster would have been averted if he had gone upstream during his earlier rescues. If he had, he would have seen the person who was throwing them into the lake! In this analogy, the allopathic doctor is the one dealing with the emergency of people drowning; the naturopathic doctor would be inclined to venture upstream to find the person who was throwing them into the lake.

Naturopaths usually define cause from a broad perspective of mind and body. The body's ailment is viewed from the holistic/'whole-istic' perspective of diet, lifestyle, and environmental factors which compromise the optimal functioning of the body. The cause of illness is regarded as a process rather than a single event.

Rather than primarily studying the nature of diseases, allopathic doctors could instead study the factors that support human health and well-being. This is what is called the salutogenic approach. A great analogy for the current situation is where we set up a system for people to master the science of success, but we primarily give them thousands of failures to study. The smart and appropriate way would be to make them study as many successful people as possible.

We have a system where the vast majority of those in the health care system did not study the factors that promote health. They instead study how to cure diseases, perform surgery, or as in the case of a pharmacist, to study how to dispense suppressant medicine. If 'health-care' practitioners had gone through a system which taught the salutogenic approach (apart from performing surgery when absolutely necessary) they would primarily be involved in giving nutritional advice, dispensing nutritional supplements, and advising clients on how to prevent disease, which usually involves paying attention to diet and lifestyle, etc. And as we know, prevention is better than trying to cure.

The salutogenic approach is not the mainstream approach, therefore the majority of us are socialised into admiring the allopathic type of medical care. We, the general public, are also socialised into looking up to and holding in high esteem the qualification that it gives to the individual. We admire doctors. Those who enter this profession also have a high regard for it. Once trained, their belief in their profession and the esteem in which they hold it grows. If you add to this the esteem that doctors receive from society and the general high levels of pay, this results in a great formula for loyalty to such a system. Who would want to diminish their doctor-status, or elevate an alternative that would threaten their job? This is not to suggest that they are doing it solely for the money. However, once any person attains a comfortable lifestyle and has dependents, such as a spouse and children, self-interest is inevitable.

Even if many doctors are inclined to endorse other forms of medicines, they are compelled legally to stay within the confines of what they were taught to get their qualification, or risk been struck-off, sued, or being sent to prison. The doctor, in effect, becomes a person who diagnoses and not a person who cures. They are not even the ones who decide what medicines are the best to treat their patients. This is because it is the drug companies that decide what options they have to choose from and therefore what medicine the patient can take. Drug companies research the drugs and bring them to the market. When you consider that there are more than eight thousand prescription medicines on the market and the majority of them were not on the market when the doctor was studying, it makes sense that they would rely on the drugs companies for information.

Do you think there is something deeply flawed in this arrangement? Is it likely to increase the inflexibility of the system? In effect, doctors have become powerless drug industry salespeople.

It is quite easy to see how a system that has become a highly intensive money generating business is also inflexible in its search for a solution.

The pharmaceutical companies that are at the forefront of investing large sums into drug research are stuck in three ruts. The first rut is that people who are involved in pharmaceutical companies are no different from the rest of us: they have been predominantly socialised into believing in allopathic medicine. Secondly, once socialised and schooled in this way, they get involved in a system in which it costs about a billion dollars to bring a drug to the market. This point is related to the fact that the production of medicine has big business considerations; allopathic medicine has mushroomed into a large commercial enterprise.

Spending a billion dollars to bring a drug to the market would surely put enormous pressure on everyone within the industry to work hard in recouping the costs, and in making a profit[5]. Thirdly, with this reality it was inevitable that there would be a realisation that dispensing medicines that are mostly suppressants is vastly profitable. It is vastly profitable because in many instances people take them for life. In effect, allopathic medicine has a high repeat ratio, thus they are able to generate large profits.

In the case of cancer, what is the nature of the primary drug treatment that has so impressed the medical industry that they find it necessary to defend it? It is vitally important that those who currently have cancer, and those who may develop it in the future, be aware of and understand the nature of the treatment options they will be presented with. It is usually a choice of chemotherapy; radiotherapy, or surgery; or two of the three, or all three taken together.

---

*Treating disease is enormously profitable, preventing disease is not. – **British Cancer Control Society***

When there are billions of dollars on the line, some people will lie.
–Anthony Robbins

---

5 If profit becomes the main priority, health will become secondary.

DEADLY CHEMOTHERAPY AND RADIATION TREATMENT

After trillions of dollars have been spent on cancer research for over a century, we have a situation where the most common treatments for cancer are chemotherapy and radiotherapy. After so many years of research and spending the extraordinary sum of money mentioned, the best that the cancer industry has come up with are drugs that kill both healthy and unhealthy cells. Isn't this incredible? Is it not also extraordinary that chemotherapy's basic characteristic – that of killing both good and bad cells – is well known, yet millions of people still queue up annually to have this treatment?

Apart from killing both good and bad cells, what else should people know about chemotherapy's effects on the body? What else should they know about this treatment that is at the forefront of fighting cancer? Here is what some doctors have had to say about this treatment:

Cancer researchers, medical journals, and the popular media all have contributed to a situation in which many people with common malignancies are being treated with drugs not known to be effective. – Dr. Martin Shapiro, UCLA

Despite widespread use of chemotherapies, breast cancer mortality has not changed in the last 70 years – (Thomas Dao, MD NEJM Mar 1975 292 p 707)

Many medical oncologists recommend chemotherapy for virtually any tumour, with a hopefulness undiscouraged by almost invariable failure.
- Albert Braverman MD *Lancet* 1991

Most cancer patients in this country die of chemotherapy. Chemotherapy does not eliminate breast, colon, or lung cancers. This fact has been documented for over a decade, yet doctors still use chemotherapy for these tumours. – Allen Levin, MD UCSF, *The Healing of Cancer.*

Part of the reason people die from chemotherapy is because the body becomes overwhelmed with these drugs/toxins in the blood. The body will always treat chemotherapy drugs as toxins because they are. Anything that enters the body has to be either assimilated or eliminated. The blood and the body become overwhelmed because the liver, kidneys and the lymphatic system, that are responsible for eliminating toxins out of the body, are unable to get rid of the toxins fast enough. So, in effect, some people die from blood poisoning, not from cancer. – Author

The *lymphatic system* is a circulatory system like our bloodstream. It carries a colorless fluid called lymphatic fluid, which travels throughout our body. It rids our body of the waste products (including old *red blood cells*) produced during daily, internal functions, thus protecting us from the harmful effects of the toxins that we would experience, otherwise. This fluid cleans our tissues and also keeps our cells well-nourished. *The lymphatic system lacks a pump to move the fluid* it carries. The pump for the blood is the heart. For lymph fluid, the flow back to the heart is achieved through a more passive process involving muscle contractions and gravity. Because of the extremely toxic nature of chemotherapy drugs, the body would benefit from a quick removal. However, the normal speed of lymphatic system drainage would not be adequate to remove them fast enough.

Now, think about this: if our body would be harmed without the removal of waste produced during *normal daily internal functions*, what is our chance of escaping harm from chemotherapy drugs that are a thousand times worse than the natural waste our body produces and which floods our system?

The inability of the liver and lymphatic system to quickly shift out the chemo drugs may not cause immediate death. However, even if death does not occur, a lengthy stay of the chemo drugs will damage the body. The body cannot be fixed as easily as a car. This is especially true in the case of organ or blood damage. So the damage cause by chemotherapy can never be justified in the course of performing a no-cure exercise. We will only continue to accept this no-cure chemotherapy if we are locked into the belief that a person will die sooner, or more harshly, without chemo treatment than with it. Most importantly, we will continue to accept this if we continue to believe that there is no better alternative than the use of this harsh, invasive, healthy-cell-killing, set of poisons.

In my introduction, I quoted the World Health Organisation (WHO) which stated that 'lack of physical activity' put us at risk of developing cancer. How does exercise help us to prevent cancer? In general, exercise increases our intake of oxygen. This is especially true of aerobic type exercises (i.e., any exercises designed to increase oxygen intake). However, another vital role that exercise plays is that it aids the lymphatic system to pump lymph fluid around the body. As already stated, this system does not have its own pump, as in the case of the bloodstream, which has the heart as its pump. Therefore, if our system has got more than the natural amount of waste, or it has unnatural toxins, exercise help the lymphatic system to pump lymph fluid around the body to do the extra cleansing work needed. A person who doesn't exercise *but has a lifestyle and diet that fills their body with too high a level of acids, toxins and poisons, which damage their cells, runs the risk of developing cancer.*

Dr. Norman McVea said, *When the body has sufficient oxygen, it is able to properly eliminate toxic wastes from the system. Natural immunity is enhanced when the system is not burdened with a heavy build-up of toxins.*

A heavy build-up of toxins is a consequence of taking chemotherapy drugs, *because they are toxins/poisons.* This is why they kill good cells and bad cells. They also compromise the immune system and therefore reduce the body's ability to eliminate toxins. This is the principle behind Dr. Levin's claim (above) that most cancer patients die from chemotherapy.

*The **Bi-Phasic Effect** is well explained by Dr Dean Black and many other researchers who were trying to figure out why tumours seemed to come back with such a vengeance after chemotherapy. Some original work was done by American Cancer Society researcher Robert Schimke in 1985, who discovered that the way cancer cells resist chemotherapy is to replicate even harder and faster.* – Dr. Tim O'Shea

Dr. Schimke is a pioneer in modern biological sciences. He has made seminal and groundbreaking contributions to at least four distinct areas of biological investigation, in some cases creating the area itself. Dr. Schimke talks about the possible effects chemotherapy might have on a tumour that otherwise may have been self-limiting:

Might such treatments convert relatively benign tumours into more lethal forms?

Chemo drugs are lethal to all cells; so the cancer cells are stimulated to try and survive any way they can, which means faster growth. In the presence of any toxin, cells will resist it to stay alive. The more they resist, the stronger they get. – Dr. Tim O'Shea

(Dr. Dean) Black sees cancer itself as just such an adaptation; a normal response to an abnormal poison. Chemotherapy simply provokes (further) adaptation. This is why we all know people who have had chemotherapy and experienced temporary remission. But when the tumour came back, it did so with a vengeance, and the patient was quickly overwhelmed. – Dr. Tim O'Shea (Author's insertions)

Every seventy seconds another American dies of cancer. That's 1,230 people every day. In 1971, such figures motivated Congress to pass the Conquest of Cancer Act. The idea behind the Act was to "declare war" on cancer – to give medical science a mandate to stop such deaths, - and the money to do it with. The sponsors of the Act hoped to eliminate cancer by 1976. – Dean Black PhD, *Cancer: Can It Be Reversed, 1990.*

Everyone should know that most cancer research is largely a fraud and that the major cancer research organisations are derelict in their duties to the people who support them. – Linus Pauling PhD (Two-time Nobel Prize winner)

(http://rense.com/general9/cre.htm)

In 1970 (the year before the Act), 17.2 percent of all deaths were from cancer. By 1980 the figure was 20 percent... Recent studies "show a steady increase in age-adjusted mortality for all kinds of cancer."

[One cancer researcher's conclusion was]: "All the [medical therapies] utilised to treat cancer... have also been demonstrated to cause cancer."... I asked myself, "If medical cancer therapies have been demonstrated to cause cancer, why do medical doctors keep using them?" –Dean Black PhD [Insertion mine]

To find out the answer to this question, he called Dr. Harry Rubin, **Professor of Molecular and Cell Biology at Berkley**, University of California, who was one of the leading scientists in this area of cancer research. Dr Black reported that Dr Rubin's response was, *"Because they don't know what else to do."*

The situation of doctors *"not knowing* what else to do" is directly related to my earlier point about doctors relying on drug companies to provide new treatments. According to Dr Black, *When Dr. Rubin says medical doctors don't know what else to do, he means that only killing can-*

cer cells makes sense to them... because they define cancer cells as vicious, destructive enemies [– mutations that are irreversible]. This is why they find it hard to imagine other options.[Author's insertions]

–Dr. Tim O'Shea wrote that: *It is startling to discover what chemotherapy drugs are made from. The first ones were made from mustard gas contained in the weapons that killed so many soldiers in WW 1, eventually outlawed by the Geneva Convention. In the 1930s, Memorial Sloan-Kettering quietly began to treat breast cancer with these mustard gas derivatives. No one was cured. More Nitrogen mustard chemotherapy trials were conducted at Yale around 1943. 160 patients were treated. No one was cured. Despite this track record, the major derivative –* **Methotrexate** *– gradually gained popularity over the decades.*

Methotrexate *has been one of the most common chemotherapy drugs for the past 25 years. The fact that it's still at the top of the list and that cancer survival has not improved during that period tells the story.* – Dr. Tim O'Shea

As Methotrexate begins to kill the body's cells, it causes bleeding ulcers, bone marrow suppression, lung damage, and kidney damage. (HSI Newsletter Apr 1999 p. 5) It also causes "severe anaemia, and has triggered or intensified cancerous tumours." (Ruesch, p. 18) Other common effects are permanent sclerosing (hardening) of the veins, blood clotting, and destruction of skin and mucous membranes. – Dr. Tim O'Shea

Cytoxan *is another of the most common chemo drugs. Besides the "normal" side effects, it causes urinary bleeding, lung disease, and heart damage. This preposterous sentence actually appears at webmd.com as a rationale for* **Cytoxan:** *"***Cytoxan*** also works by decreasing your immune system's response to various diseases."*

And decreasing response to disease is going to benefit any patient exactly how...??? They can print ridiculous sentences like this largely because no-

body reads them. Most patients sheepishly accept whatever drugs the doctor dreams up, without question. It's truly marketing from heaven – unquestioned compliance, even if ordered to commit suicide. –Dr. Tim O'Shea

Chemotherapy drugs ... *may also harm normal cells, including cells in the mouth. Side effects include problems with your teeth and gums; the soft, moist lining of your mouth; and the glands that make saliva (spit)... You are more likely to get an infection [as a side effect in the mouth], which can be dangerous when you are receiving cancer treatment. The side effects can hurt and make it hard to eat, talk, and swallow.* –National Institute of Dental and Craniofacial Research (NIDCR) [Insertions mine]

I think that it's easy for those who care about the epidemic of cancer to verify the side effects of chemotherapy. One aspect that does not require verification is the fact that many lose their hair during treatment. It is also a fact that some people's teeth have been known to fall out. Should we regard this as a 'clue' as to what other damage this 'treatment' does to the body? Read the further information about chemotherapy below. This information should let you, at minimum, question the reason that such a drug largely goes unchallenged in the public domain. The following is an extensive extract taken from an online article written by Dr. Tim O'Shea:

CHEMOTHERAPY: AN UNPROVEN PROCEDURE

How can that be true of the #1 cancer treatment in the U.S. for the past 50 years? The plain fact is, no legitimate scientific studies or clinical trials independent of the companies selling chemo drugs have ever proven chemotherapy's effectiveness, except in a small percentage of very rare types of cancer. For solid tumours of adults, the vast majority of cancer, or anything that has metastasized, chemotherapy simply doesn't work.

If one is going to even begin to look at the legitimate research regarding the failure of mainstream cancer therapies, all that initial research was done

by Ralph Moss, and elaborated very clearly in his two books The Cancer Industry and Questioning Chemotherapy. Even though they were written in the 90s, the fundamental objections to the philosophy behind chemotherapy are timeless. Cancer therapy has simply not advanced in the past 20 years enough to make Moss' work anything but essential reading for learning about the ongoing problems with mainstream cancer treatment. Moss didn't really continue his research at that level after that initial effort, but these two books remain as landmarks in the field.

When he was researching his first book, Dr Moss uncovered the shocking research of a German epidemiologist from the Heidelberg/Mannheim Tumour Clinic, named Dr. Ulrich Abel. This Dr Abel did a comprehensive review and analysis of every major study and clinical trial of chemotherapy ever done. His conclusions should be read by anyone who is about to embark on the Chemo Express. To make sure he had reviewed everything ever published on chemotherapy, Abel sent letters to over 350 medical centres around the world asking them to send him anything they had published on the subject. Abel researched thousands of articles: it is unlikely that anyone in the world knows more about chemotherapy than he did.

The analysis took Abel two years, but the results are astounding: Abel found that the overall worldwide success rate of chemotherapy was "appalling" because there was simply no scientific evidence available anywhere that chemotherapy can "extend in any appreciable way the lives of patients suffering from the most common organic cancers."

Abel emphasizes that chemotherapy rarely can improve the quality of life. He describes chemotherapy as "a scientific wasteland" and states that at least 80 percent of chemotherapy administered throughout the world is worthless, and is akin to the "emperor's new clothes" – neither doctor nor patient is willing to give up on chemotherapy even though there is no scientific evidence that it works! – Lancet 10 Aug 91 [35]

No mainstream media even mentioned this comprehensive study: it was totally buried.

Similar are the conclusions of most medical researchers who actually try to work their way past the smoke and mirrors to get to the real statistics. In evaluating a therapeutic regimen, the only thing that really matters is death rate – will a treatment significantly extend a patient's life? Not life as a vegetable, but the natural healthy independent lifespan of a human being.

Media stories and most articles in medical journals go to great lengths to hide the true numbers of people dying from cancer, by talking about other issues. In 'Questioning Chemotherapy', Moss talks about several of the ways they do it:

Response rate *is a favourite.*

If a dying patient's condition changes even for a week or a month, especially if the tumour shrinks temporarily, the patient is listed as having "responded to" chemotherapy. No joke! The fact that the tumour comes back stronger soon after chemo is stopped is not figured into the equation. The fact that the patient has to endure horrific side effects in order to temporarily shrink the tumour is not considered. The fact that the patient soon dies is not figured into the equation. The idea is to sell, sell, and sell. Sell chemotherapy.

Also in the media we find the loud successes chemotherapy has had on certain rare types of cancer, like childhood leukaemia, and Hodgkin's lymphoma. But for the vast majority of cancer cases, chemo is a failure, worse yet, a toxic one.

Even with Hodgkins, one of chemo's much-trumpeted triumphs, the cure is frequently a success, but the patient dies. He just doesn't die of Hodgkin's disease, that's all. In the 1994 Journal of the National Cancer Institute, they published a 47-year study of more than 10,000 patients with

*Hodgkin's lymphoma, who were treated with chemotherapy. Even though there was success with the Hodgkin's itself, these patients encountered an incidence of leukaemia that was **six times** the normal rate. This is a very common type of reported success within the cancer industry – again, the life of the patient is not taken into account.*

*Another thing is, in evaluating any treatment, there must be a **risk/benefit analysis** – a carefully standardized protocol for measuring the actual risks vs. the proven, unvarnished positive outcomes from the procedure being studied. This is a very fundamental part of the scientific method.*

Due to the gigantic economic pressures fearful of the results, such evaluation has been systematically put aside in the U.S. chemotherapy industry for the past 40 years. Primarily because a favourable report would be impossible, considering the toxic nature of the drugs involved. This extract was taken from the following website: www.thedoctorwithin.com

THE DIFFICULTY OF CHANGING PEOPLE'S MINDS

It is not very easy to change people's minds about their choice of medicine. This is true especially when the medicine is endorsed by a government. Furthermore, the use of medicine is an emotional issue, because it is intertwined with our deepest vulnerabilities – the fear of ill health and the fear of death. My first-hand experience with this inflexibility was a very painful one, because it involved my aunt. The extent to which a person can become inflexible in their thinking is always an astonishing thing to observe. This inflexibility is based on the blank slate principle. This principle simply states that at birth the mind is almost empty and, like a computer, it needs software to function. It is indifferent to what 'software' is planted in it. So, whatever was implanted in the mind becomes the template for action. People will always adhere to their beliefs, depending on how emotionally powerful they are. People's belief and trust in a particular medicine will be similar to their belief in other powerful beliefs such as politics and spirituality, and therefore will cause a similar adherence.

Some years ago my aunt was diagnosed with breast cancer. They removed the breast and eventually gave her the 'all clear'. The cancer returned a couple of years later in a different location. This time it was more aggressive. I tried to get her to consider alternative treatment but she showed little interest. She was listed for surgery, so I supplied her with information about an approach that didn't involve surgery. She had the surgery and died shortly after. What should have been her analysis of the situation before agreeing to surgery for a second time? She could have said to herself, "It is either they lied about my being 'all cleared' of cancer, or they were incompetent." If she had reasoned it out in this manner, she would at least have had a look at an alternative approach, but she never did. She was one of tens of millions of people who are socialised into absolute belief in this type of medicine. Such faith was never, and never will be, rewarded. Millions of such people are no longer with us, who, perhaps, would have been with us today.

So we find ourselves in a situation where, in spite of the absence of a cure after over a hundred years of research, trillions of dollars spent and the undoubted harm caused to the body by chemotherapy and radiation treatment, many will resist looking in a new direction. The majority of people involved in the medical industry are fixated in the belief that the solution for the body's cure is within scientific methods of a laboratory nature. In simple language, they see medicine as something that is designed in a lab. Yet they will often take the basis of these medicines from Nature and turn it into a drug. Apparently, our knowledge is always greater than Nature, and Nature *always* needs modification!

In reality, scientists are often governed by the need to protect what they discover or invent by a patent. And for a drug to qualify for a patent, it has criteria to meet. A medicine is patentable based upon the extent to which it has a unique synthetic combination of chemicals. If a new drug has even trace elements of an old drug it is not patentable. So the growth of the pharmaceutical industry is funded by constantly inventing new drugs.

The need to have patentable drugs hinders the drug companies' ability to provide a solution to the cancer epidemic. Without a legal framework to protect their drugs, it would not be economically viable to spend billions of dollars to do the research and development, then bring them to the market, recoup their costs and make a profit, as well as stay in business by supplying an international market. Without a patent for their drugs, all the countries that accept the value of such drugs would simply make their own.

There are thousands of drugs on the market, but there are not thousands of herbs or 'foods' that Nature produces that are compatible with the human body. A synthetic combination of chemicals cannot cure any disease; it can only suppress the symptoms of the disease! This is not debatable since none of the major diseases are said to be curable. People take medication for their entire lives and die without their body ever returning to its former glory.

This is the reality that many of us have accepted as 'normal' because we have been socialised into accepting the symbols of allopathic medicine as representations of advanced medicine. So, if someone doesn't wear a white coat or carry a stethoscope, s/he is not a doctor. The other trappings of the allopathic medical system include various sophisticated machines, needles to withdraw blood for testing, and the means to do urine tests.

These trappings of medicine are relatively new to the long history of human civilisations which dates back at least 8000 years. Yet in spite of all this modern equipment, disease and illness are at epidemic proportions, and deaths from the major diseases are not slowing down. In the United Kingdom, the health service is under enormous strain to cope, and to provide adequate 'care'. So what were we using before we invented these machines? How did we cure diseases before we learnt surgery?

My experience with an expert, Chinese, herbal medicine and acupuncture practitioner should provide a clue. After almost destroying my body by abusing it with a poor diet, I developed many problems, one of which was irritable bowel syndrome (IBS). After being diagnosed at the hospital, I was prescribed tablets, and a sachet containing a powdery substance – both to take after meals. How long was I supposed to do this? This could have been a lifetime activity. However, the main point is that I wasn't experiencing any improvement.

I decided that I didn't want to live like this for the rest of my life. I found a Chinese-herbal and acupuncture practitioner, and thus began eleven years of restoring my body to health. I now do not have IBS, and my health has dramatically improved. A change of diet and other herbal supplements have also been crucial in my transformation. Now, before you question the length of time it took to achieve this, remember that most people take medicines for a lifetime *without* transforming their health! You can also bear in mind that poor health and illness is progressive; it does not occur overnight. After poor health, good health and well being is also progressive; it may take weeks, months or years.

In addition to all that I gained physically from my time with Dr. Lee, other benefits came from experiencing his method of diagnosing. During all the years of my being diagnosed and treated by Dr. Lee, I never had to take a blood or urine test. He would look at my tongue and in my eyes with one of those doctors' flashlights and this was the full extent of his equipment. However, his most amazing 'equipment' was his hands. He would place his fingers on the pulse of my wrists every week. From this he could tell me what my condition was at that time. How did I know he was accurate? I knew because although he never asked me any questions, he was always aware when I had an infection. Since I'm always aware when I have the onset of flu, I was able to prove that his scientific method was correct. If I went to any GP, they would not be able to diagnose me as coming down with the flu, not unless I was displaying symptoms. No equipment or test would help them in this regard either.

Chinese medicine is older than western medicine. Yet, Dr. Lee told me that they had herbs that are effective at dealing with cancer, but they are not allowed to make use of them in their practice. I am not saying this to advocate Chinese medicine as a solution for cancer. The nature of the disease does not seem to dictate a single solution or panacea. I've simply told part of my story to provoke you to think outside the box, or better still, to get rid of the box entirely. Most diseases are a result of poor diet and lifestyle habits. In these cases a cure always has two parts: changing our diet and lifestyle and nourishing our body back to health. The question is, should we nourish it back to health with food and Nature's herbs or should we use drugs?

The medical research and pharmaceutical industries will not be able to come up with a cure for cancer, within the paradigm described, because of the cause and nature of this disease. The nature of the disease is such that no 'one' miracle drug or herb will cure it. To repeat, there will never be a panacea. First and foremost, cancer is the result of a *process* caused by diet, lifestyle and environment. The cure is to reverse the process of whatever combination of factors caused the cancer. This involves changing diet and lifestyle, and taking herbs and nutrients that are capable of restoring the body back to a healthy alkaline pH balance. Such a healthy pH balance will improve the intelligent body's effectiveness in dealing with cancerous cells, without harming the body the way chemotherapy does. Chemotherapy kills both good and bad cells. If your body has lots of bad cells, why would you want to kill *any* of your healthy cells? This would be a time when you should be desperate to keep all your healthy cells!

If a healthy person takes chemotherapy they will become sick; what is the chance of a sick person taking it and becoming well? – Dr. Llaila Afrika (naturopath)

Dr. Warburg's experiments and conclusions have now been vindicated by what you'll read in the next chapter. In the following quote he made the claim that cancer should not still be shrouded in mystery. This quote is an excerpt from an article based on a lecture delivered at Stuttgart on May 25, 1955, before the German Central Committee for Cancer Control. It was first published in German [Naturwissenschaften 42, 401 (1955)]. This translation was prepared by Dean Burk, Jehu Hunter and W.H. Everhardy of the US Department of Health, Education and Welfare, Public Health Service, National Institutes of Health, Bethesda, MD:

The era in which the fermentation of the cancer cells or its importance could be disputed is over, and no-one today can doubt that we understand the origin of cancer cells if we know how their large fermentation originates, or, to express it more fully, if we know how the damaged respiration and the excessive fermentation of the cancer cells originate...

... But nobody today can say that one does not know what cancer and its prime cause {are}. On the contrary, there is no disease whose prime cause is better known, so that today ignorance is no longer an excuse that one cannot do more about prevention.

That the prevention of cancer will come, there is no doubt, for man wishes to survive. But how long prevention will be avoided depends on how long the prophets of agnosticism will succeed in inhibiting the application of scientific knowledge in the cancer field. In the meantime, millions of men [and women] must die of cancer unnecessarily.
(http://www.oxygenhealingtherapies.com/Medical_Ozone_Cancer.html)

Are you now convinced about the basic cause of cancer? If you're still not convinced about the merit of my reasoning and that of all those quoted, you should have no doubt after you read the information below. After reading it, you should realise that the only difference between the naturopaths' position and the cancer industry is what one will do with the indisputable facts about the nature of cancer. Based on the information below, the cause of cancer should no longer be in dispute. I leave it to you to decide which point of view holds the best solution.

CHAPTER THREE

THE EXPERIMENT THAT INDICATED THE CURE
COMES FULL CIRCLE

Dr. Warburg's experiment was done in 1924, yet amazingly, it seems to have taken until 2009 for that information to reach the mainstream media. That is about eighty five years! The Sunday Express published a 'landmark' article written by Jo Willey, their Health Correspondent, entitled "Oxygen Kills Cancer" on Sunday, August 2nd, 2009. She cited the source and basis of the information as, *The research, published today in the journal Cancer Research, was carried out by scientists from the Cancer Research UK–MRC Gray Institute for Radiation Oncology & Biology at the University of Oxford. They treated mice with certain drugs that improved the stability of blood vessels in the tumours.*

(http://www.express.co.uk/news/uk/117617/Oxygen-kills-cancer)

The article declared, 'A NEW way of destroying cancer, radically increasing effectiveness of radiotherapy, was last night heralded as a "very exciting" breakthrough by scientists.'

Why would this be a new 'breakthrough' in light of the Warburg experiment from 1924? The article went on to say:

Previously experts have tried to cut off the blood supply, fuelling tumour growth to starve and kill it. But the new method improves the blood vessels within the tumour, increasing the concentration of oxygen... If the oxygen supply within a tumour is increased, cancerous cells become far more sensitive to treatment.

This is a confirmation that oxygen deprivation is the root cause of cancer. The information in this article is also an admission that scientists had been going in the wrong direction, and that doing so was the opposite of what the Warburg experiment demonstrated nearly ninety years ago. He demonstrated that *oxygen deprivation* causes a series of reactions including the mutation of cells that become cancerous and the switching to fermentation of glucose/sugar to produce energy. Despite this they went in the direction of trying to starve cancer cells of oxygen, which is the very thing that causes cells to become cancerous! It took them this long to realise that this doesn't make sense? Wow!

So now they have 'discovered' the effect that oxygen has on cancer cells, they now want to give them oxygen. Perhaps we can safely assume that all this time it had escaped their notice that oxygen gives life to human beings! This is what the article stated concerning what scientists have now 'noticed' about the effect that oxygen has on tumours:

Instead of boosting a tumour's growth potential, it (oxygen) has the opposite effect and weakens the cancer from the inside, making it far more sensitive to harsh radiotherapy.

So now that they have 'discovered' the marvellous effect that oxygen has on cancer cells, their 'solution' is *to continue* applying treatments that kill good and bad cells, and to inflict the devastating side effects that I've already listed. The *harsh radiotherapy* is still one of their top choices of treatment. In effect, nothing has changed. This 'discovery' has not inspired them to look in a different direction for a solution.

This fact is one of the most powerful demonstrations of how people can be locked into a paradigm. Worse, it shows how people can be dominated by powerful self-interest. This continued use of radiotherapy and chemotherapy is an indication of a very rigid system.

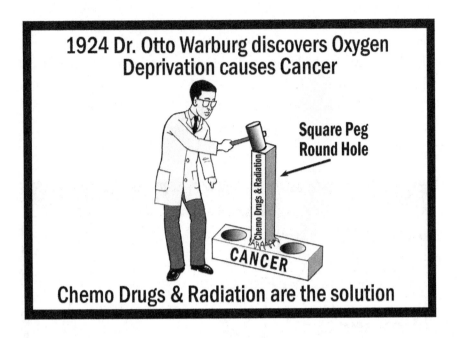

The 'new breakthrough' on the role of oxygen deprivation in causing cancer has caused a reaction that is tantamount to saying: "We've once again discovered that the hole is round, however, we are going to continue to try and 'ram' a square peg into it." In effect, they are going to continue with their method of burning out the symptoms without correcting the cause. Therefore, even if this 'discovery' makes them more effective at destroying cancer cells, the 'benefits' to the patient will be the same. They will have internal scars and damages; they will suffer the anguish of waiting for the outcome of the unquantifiable and mysterious 'remission' period, and all without knowledge of the various factors that can cause a return of this dreaded disease. So, at minimum, the fear of cancer will remain. Fear breeds stress, and stress is not conducive to good health or a high quality of life.

As I previously stated, Dr. O'Shea, who is opposed to chemotherapy, has this to say about its effect on cancer: *Some original work was done by American Cancer Society researcher Robert Schimke in 1985, who discovered that the way cancer cells resist chemotherapy, is to replicate even harder and faster.*

The article, in the Sunday Express, also went on to admit that cancer cells are resistant to radiotherapy:

Usually cancer cells fight to survive, but the new treatment makes them weak and less resistant to treatment. Cancers low in oxygen are three times more resistant to radiotherapy. So, by restoring oxygen levels to that of a normal cell, the tumours become three times more sensitive to treatment. And a better, more stable blood supply in the tumour enables improved delivery of chemotherapy drugs.

The characteristic of cancer cells 'fighting to survive' and 'becoming stronger' is consistent with the quotes in chapter two from Dr. Tim O'Shea regarding Dean Black's findings called the **Bi-Phasic Effect,** which explained why tumours seemed to come back with such a vengeance after chemotherapy. Dr. Tim O'Shea also stated that, *"We all know people who have had chemotherapy and experienced temporary remission. But when the tumour came back, it did so with a vengeance, and the patient was quickly overwhelmed."*

If you examine closely what is said above, it implies the alarming consequence of continued use of chemotherapy and radiotherapy. If cancer cells are known to grow stronger and spread faster because of these drugs, what is to prevent the same thing from continuing to happen? If *cancer cells resist chemotherapy* by replicating harder and faster, these drugs therefore make the situation worse and speed up the person's death! Yet they continue to use this dangerous drugs approach because, as always, they are *hoping* to kill all the cancer cells and leave none to proliferate – the Russian roulette approach. The fact that most people do *not* survive, is proof that this approach doesn't work. We've been brainwashed to accept these dangerous treatments and their extremely poor ratio of successful results.

In spite of the 'new' discovery, its approach to solving the cancer epidemic, because of the prevailing medical culture, does not deal with the underlying reason that a person's body develops cancer in the first place. In other words, the dietary (highly acidic) and lifestyle factors that create the environment that supports cancer growth within the body are never dealt with. So, despite this new approach, these underlying factors will remain the same after the body is weakened by chemotherapy and/or radiation treatment. Cancer cells that escape being killed by chemotherapy and radiation treatment will find it easy to return 'with a vengeance' in such an environment. And even if all cancer cells were killed, if the underlying causes remain the same, the person will be prone to a return of cancer. *It is also highly unlikely that chemotherapy or radiation treatment will kill all cancer cells, because once a person has developed cancer, it gets into the blood, and once it gets into the blood, it's all over the body.* However, the treatment is usually focussed on which organ(s) the cancer appears to be in clusters.

Throughout my research I did not see or hear any evidence to justify the impression that the cancer found in different parts of the body is distinctively unique and therefore require a different cure. The article in the Sunday Express confirms this, as you will read below. This impression of distinctively different cancers is created by those who interpret cancer in this way, and these are the same people who are unable to resolve its treatment. This has resulted in them soliciting for donations to fund cancer research based upon it being in various parts of the body. Cancer that is visibly clustered in the breast is called breast cancer. This is one of the 'types' of cancer that is given special mention for the funding of 'special research'. Another is the cancer that forms clusters in the prostate, called prostate cancer.

I have found that the basic reason as to why cells become cancerous is the same, irrespective of whether the cells are part of our lungs, prostrate, breast, liver, or any other part of the body. Yet we have a situation where there are specialists for treating cancer in different parts of the body.

All of our cells, irrespective of the organ they are located in, have the same need for oxygen and will therefore react in the same way if starved of oxygen. The evidence suggests that cancer in different locations of the body has the same basic characteristics and is caused by the same processes. The earlier article in the Sunday Express confirms the basic nature of all cancers by elaborating on what benefits were hoped to be gained by giving oxygen to cancer cells: *Research was carried out on breast, head and neck cancers as well as carcinomas that line the surface of the skin and organs. But it is hoped the treatment will be as effective in **all radiotherapy-treated tumours, including those notoriously hard to treat such as pancreatic cancer.*** (Bold for my emphasis)

The promotion of the idea that cancers in different locations are uniquely different [and require different treatment], such as breast and prostate cancer has totally misled the public. This idea gives the impression that a person's breast, for example, can have a genetic make-up that makes it predisposed to getting cancer. This has led to tragic consequences whereby people have been known, for example, to have a mastectomy as a pre-emptive measure against getting breast cancer. In this scenario, the person accepts that the breast is the primary target for them to get cancer. This is based on the gene theory, and totally ignores, or demote the role that diet or lifestyle plays in the person getting cancer. This theory seems to suggest that a perfectly healthy person can have a genetic make-up or 'cancer-gene' that is likely to trigger the formation of cancer in their body and kill them. I am contending that there is no such thing as a 'cancer-gene' that causes cancer. This theory ignores all the proven factors that facilitate cancer growth, such oxygen deprivation, acidity, and carbon dioxide. No proof has been *demonstrated* of this theory.

Why do they heavily promote breast and prostate cancer? The fact that they are very common doesn't make them unique. Are they doing this because these organs are associated with sex, and therefore easily elicit an emotional response in their drive to solicit money for research? *People do not die from breast or prostate cancer of themselves.* For death to occur, the cancer has to spread to organ(s) that are critical to the sustaining of life. We can survive without breast or prostate. If you thought that people literally die from breast or prostate cancer, it is because this is the common and misleading impression that is given by the cancer industry.

It seems that this segregation of cancer is caused by the level of difficulty involved in treating cancer in some locations. This difficulty arises from the scorch and burn characteristic of the chemo and radiation treatment, and is dependent on how vital and how delicate the organ is. The pancreas is an organ that has very limited powers of recovery, therefore, it can be described as being delicate, hence it is known to be one that is *notoriously hard to treat*. However, now they have a 'breakthrough' that shows that even this *notoriously hard to treat* cancer responds positively to the wonderful breath of oxygen! If cancer in all locations react positively to oxygen, does it make sense that they all have the same characteristics?

On the *Cancer Research UK* website another article posted on March 1, 2012, has the headline, 'New clue to how cancer cells beat oxygen starvation'. The article started with the declaration: *We need oxygen to survive. Even the cells in the deepest, darkest parts of our body can't live without it. But some cancer cells adapt to survive in very low oxygen levels, and these end up being some of the most difficult to treat…scientists in labs around the world are working to uncover the molecular machinery that allows cells to do this.* (http://scienceblog.cancerresearchuk.org/2012/03/01/new-clue-to-how-cancer-cells-beat-oxygen-starvation/)

The headline and the body of the article seem to suggest that the starvation of oxygen is something that happens *after* the cells become cancerous. This is a position that is opposite to the findings of Dr. Otto Warburg's experiment which state that oxygen starvation triggers (cause) the formation of cancer. However, in spite of the seemingly opposite view, the article confirms that oxygen starvation or hypoxia is a critical factor in the cancer problem.

Interestingly, hypoxia is also defined as, 'Oxygen deficiency causing a very strong drive to correct the deficiency'. What did Dr. Warburg's experiment revealed as to how mutated cells respond to a deficiency in oxygen? They switch to the fermentation of glucose/sugar for the production of energy, and this process generates more carbon dioxide (CO_2) than normal cell respiration. The Cancer Research UK article did not mention CO_2, but stated, *"Cancer cells have evolved to beat these conditions (starvation of oxygen) by switching on a protein called hypoxia-inducible factor (HIF). The HIF response encourages new blood vessels to grow around and into the tumour. It also helps the tumour to adapt to hypoxic conditions by **using alternative methods to produce energy*** (My insertion for clarity and bold for emphasis). Do you recognize the similarity with Dr. Warburg's findings? It is further confirmation of the essential characteristics of cancer. The difference is the sequencing and interpretation of the information.

No drugs or herbs can change the underlying cause(s) of cancer. Only a change in diet and lifestyle will do this. – Author

---

THE LIFESTYLE THAT BECOMES THE SOLUTION: AN ALTERNATIVE APPROACH TO OVERCOMING THE CANCER EPIDEMIC.

Hopefully you are, at least, discouraged from using 'chemical treatments' and you are now inspired to consider an alternative approach that is not harmful to the body. It is time for people to stop accepting what is known as *Brown's paradox*: medicines that are supposed to help but harm the body at the same time. I think this is an inane approach to medicine and the care of our body.

Populations eating an animal-based diet are plagued with cancer, and those eating plant-based diets are not – The Rave Diet

The overwhelming message that I wish to gain traction is that we cannot continue to use chemotherapy and radiotherapy to treat cancer. These chemical and radiation treatments cannot remain unchallenged, because they have clearly become a major part of the problem. If this is about saving people's lives and returning them to good health, then alternative approaches have to be *extensively* tried. It is clear that alternatives have to come from a source outside of the cocoon of the cancer industry. The self-interest and methodology that is imbedded within the cancer industry makes it unsuited to solve this threat to the human population. *We cannot be worse off if we do not use chemicals that have so many dangerous side effects.*

Don't look to the cancer industry for a cure. The cure for cancer is right inside of you. And the only way to win your personal war on cancer is to strengthen your immune system by changing your diet. Plants foods are the only foods that strengthen the immune system, and contain cancer fighting nutrients. So a change to a plant based diet turns out to be the only real cure for cancer we have. The strongest cancer fighting medicines on the planet don't have scary names, and they are not found in hospitals, but in your humble grocery store. – The Rave Diet (DVD documentary)

Natural herbs and foods are not fads within the arena of medicine. The body is also a natural organism! – Author

---

Naturopathic doctors are also claiming that there are herbs, in the form of herbal supplements, that are good at taking oxygen to the cells and that these herbs also have natural cancer fighting chemicals. This is the same claim that my Chinese-herbal doctor made, as I mentioned earlier. The herbal approach is an anathema to the cancer industry because herbs are not patentable! This need for patentable drugs is part of the reason the cancer industry is ineffective. As I've already stated, for a medicine to qualify for a patent is the extent to which it has *a unique synthetic combination of chemicals. If a new drug has even trace elements of an old drug it is not patentable.*

You do not have to be a scientist to accept that the body prefers natural substances to synthetic substances. Let me remind you of a simple wisdom: if a healthy person takes chemotherapy, they will become ill. Therefore, how can a sick person take it and become well?

The ancient Egyptian doctor, Imhotep, is credited with saying: "Let your food be your medicine, and your medicine be your food." In modern medical history, Hippocrates is credited with saying the same thing.

The link between disease and deficiencies in our diet has been known for a very long time. The disease of scurvy is one such example. If you take into consideration the severe nature of this disease, you may be surprised at the simplicity of the cure.

The initial symptoms of scurvy usually manifest as misery and depression with constant fatigue, followed by formation of spots on the skin, around the hair follicles, mainly on the shins; pain in the limbs; and later, swollen and spongy gums, vulnerable to bleeding; loose teeth; and severe pain in the joints caused by bleeding within them. Left untreated, scurvy can lead to festering wounds, jaundice, fever, and death.

Scurvy was common among European sailors and pirates of the 15th to the 18th centuries who sailed long voyages without sufficient fruits and vegetables on board their ships. Many of them frequently perished from the condition. Although a rare disease nowadays, anyone whose diet lacks sufficient vitamin C (ascorbic acid) can get it.

So what was the cure for this 'major' disease? The cure was vitamin C or ascorbic acid, which is found in abundance within citrus and other fruits, and vegetables!

The above illustrates a clear link between disease and nutritional deficiency. This is an example of the *science of the body* screaming out the following message: *Fruits and vegetables are meals; they are not just dress-*

ings or desserts. If this is not your current philosophy, I would suggest you make it a mantra that you repeat frequently until it translates into your eating practice. This philosophy should become a global mantra.

I've mentioned that the human body is intelligent. A disease is one of the ways in which the body tells us that we are doing something that is incompatible with its wellbeing. Vomiting is another way in which the body warns us of our ignorance. Scurvy is the result of a nutritional neglect of vitamin C, as mentioned above. Anaemia is due to insufficient iron. Deficiencies in vitamins, minerals, or other nutrients will diminish our health or cause illnesses that are actually felt. Cancer is just another symptom of the mistreatment of our bodies. It's another way of the intelligent body telling us that we are doing something that is incompatible with its wellbeing.

Ancient Africans and other indigenous people were said to have lived an average of well in excess of a hundred years. There is a group of people called the Hunzas who live in the Himalayas and who currently live, on average, above a hundred years. All these people have in common the fact that they live on whole, unprocessed foods and very little meat. A study of the diet and lifestyle of the Hunzas was carried out by Dr. Robert McCarrison, who headed the nutrition research department for the government of India. His findings are taken from the book, *The Secret Life of Plants* (1973) by Peter Tompkins and Christopher Bird:

McCarrison was struck by the fact that the Hunzas...not only could walk 120 miles at a stretch in the roughest mountain country in the world, or cut two holes in a frozen lake and swim from one to the other under the ice for the fun of it, but, with the exception of an occasional eye inflammation due to badly ventilated fires in their huts, were wholly free from disease and lived to a great age. McCarrison also found the Hunzas' health to be matched by their superior intelligence, wit, and urbanity... and though they were numerically few and their neighbours warlike, they were rarely attacked – because they always won.

As neighbouring people living in the same climate and geographical conditions were afflicted with many diseases which never appeared among the Hunzas, McCarrison began a comparative study of the dietary practices of Gilgit Agency people which then extended to various groups all over India. By feeding diverse Indian diets to rats – foolish enough to eat whatever humans will eat – McCarrison found that his rats reflected the conditions of growth, physique, and health of the people eating the same foods. Those rats which ate the diets of the peoples such as the Pathans and Sikhs increased their body weight much faster and were much healthier than those rats ingesting the daily fare of peoples like Kanarese and Bengalis. When offered the food of the Hunzas, which was limited to grain, vegetables, and fruits, along with un-pasteurized goat milk and the butter made from it, the rodents appeared to McCarrison the healthiest ever raised in his laboratory. They grew rapidly, were apparently never ill, mated with enthusiasm, and had healthy offspring.

When they were killed and autopsied at twenty-seven months – the equivalent of fifty-five years in humans – nothing whatsoever was wrong with their organs. Most amazing to McCarrison was the fact that, "throughout their lifetimes, they were gentle, affectionate, and playful."

In contrast to these 'Hunza rats', others contracted precisely the diseases of the people whose diets they were being fed and even seemed to adopt certain of their behavioural characteristics. Illnesses revealed at autopsy filled a whole page. All parts of their bodies, from womb and ovary to skin, hair, and blood, respiratory, urinary, digestive, nervous and cardio-vascular systems were afflicted. Moreover, many of them, snarling and vicious, had to be kept apart if they were not to kill each other.

The book goes on to say: *The startling evidence of McCarrison seemed to have no effect on the health authorities of the major countries of the world.*

In 1949, Dr. Elmer Nelson, in charge of nutrition at the U.S. Food and Drug Administration, was reported by the Washington Post to have made the astonishing declaration in court that: .

It is wholly unscientific to state that a well-fed body is more able to resist disease than a less well-fed body. My over-all opinion is that there has not been enough experimentation to prove that dietary deficiencies make one more susceptible to disease.'

So, after all this time, it is obvious that we still have cultures that don't recognise food as medicine, even though food, by definition, should have all the ingredients necessary to maintain health and sustain life. If this is so, it makes sense that these same ingredients would be capable of defending the body against diseases. We largely don't recognise food as medicines because we consider everything we put in our mouths as food. It's hard to consider biscuits as medicine. Because everything we put into our mouths is given the broad definition of 'food', we rarely make the distinction between 'live' foods and 'dead' foods.

The wise adage that we should let our medicine be our food, and our food be our medicine refers to 'live-food', and 'live-food' mainly refers to uncooked fruits, vegetables and nuts. Live foods are *oxygen-rich foods, and oxygen is our primary source of energy.* These foods that Nature grows also have the awesome power of the sun within them; plus the power of water; the power of vitamins and minerals; the power of proteins; the power of carbohydrates; the power of active enzymes, and the power of many other living substances that Nature deems necessary to sustain life. They are alive because if we plant them, they will grow. On the other hand, meat and refined carbohydrates do not have the same raw, live energy within them, therefore they cannot grow. These are substances that require the body to use its own energy to break them down and extract whatever little they offer.

THE PROTEIN MYTH

Protein is in all food substances. As I've already stated, you will see it listed as a nutritional content on a box of orange juice. We have been mis-educated about the amount of protein we need to be healthy. Nature tells us that baby humans are best served with the modest level of 5% protein found in their mother's milk. Babies grow more rapidly, than at any other period in their lives, on this modest amount of protein. This indicates that the idea that we need lots of protein to grow is a myth. If we grow at our most rapid on breast milk that has only 5% protein, it is telling us that we humans need very little protein in our diets. However, our protein requirements do not need to come from animal products. You may be surprised to learn that there are many vegetables that contain more protein than meat. Here are a few examples of vegetable foods compared with beef:

- Beef   28%
- Lentils   29%
- Broad beans 32%
- Almonds   12%
- Tomatoes   20%

All of these food substances have more protein than we need to be healthy, yet it has been heavily pushed that we need lots of protein to be healthy, and that this protein has to come from meat and dairy products.

More people die today of too much food than of too little. –John Kenneth Galbraith ('The Affluent Society', 1958)

What about if we approach how to eliminate cancer from the opposite angle? Why not start with eliminating what is causing the cells to mutate in the first place? We could start by eliminating the high animal-cholesterol and acidic diet with its processed carbohydrates, poisons such as alcohol, and those derived from smoking and food chemicals (preservatives, and others). An acidic body is fertile ground for cancer to grow. Cancer cells proliferate in an acidic medium; therefore, it makes sense to transform the body to a more alkaline state. Is there any evidence that an intense infusion of alkaline promoting foods can reverse the process of cancer? Yes, there is evidence.

In the November, 2000 issue of The Metro was published the story of Teresa Kay, a former TV director from Oxford, England, who was given a 50-50 chance of surviving lymph gland cancer known as a lymphoma. She shunned conventional chemotherapy and practiced, instead, what is known as the Gerson Therapy. This involves a diet that included weekly kilograms of carrots, leeks and lettuces and a kilo of garlic. These vegetables and hourly drinks of fruit juice were used to rebuild her body. To remind you, fruits and vegetables are meals!

The extent to which many of us are locked into a paradigm of chemical medicines being the solution to disease was again highlighted by Teresa Kay's statement that: *People in the medical profession thought I was mad.* As you may recall, this method (the Gerson Therapy) was listed as one of the unproven ones by the American Cancer Society and the FDA. I posted this same article on a Facebook page in support of the late Christopher Hitchens' battle against cancer. I was summarily abused by several persons for posting such 'nonsense'.

The Gerson Therapy is said to not permit the use of salt, pepper, coffee, tea, wine, processed foods, fats, butter, carbohydrate or protein. Its aim is to detoxify and boost the body nutritionally, by introducing large amounts of potassium which is largely found in fruits and vegetables, and removing the excess sodium largely found in salted and animal foods. This is said to enable the body's own immune system to fight off malignancies.

The carbohydrate or protein nutrients that the Gerson therapy refers to as not being permitted would not apply to those found in unprocessed live foods, such as almonds. – Author

---

The fact that Teresa Kay was given a 50-50 chance of survival suggests that the cancer in her lymph glands (or lymph nodes) was at a very advanced stage, so she was recommended to have chemotherapy. Lymph gland cancer is when one has cancer in the very system which is a part of the body's defence. This has to be regarded as a serious breach of the body's ability to defend itself.

With the allopathic medical treatment of cancer, doctors will sometimes remove lymph nodes that have become cancerous. This practice, I feel, can only stand up to reason if they were the ones who designed the body in the first place, and are therefore qualified to decide that *all* the lymph nodes are not necessary for good health. In reality, according to the American Cancer Society:

Nodes that have been removed during cancer surgery can leave that part of the body without a way to drain off excess fluid in the affected area. Many of the lymph vessels now run into a dead end where the node used to be, and fluid can back up. This is called lymphoedema, and it can become a lifelong problem. The more lymph nodes removed, the more likely it is to occur.

Considering chemotherapy's reputation for damaging our cells and organs, bouts of aggressive chemo treatments would surely have caused damage to her lymph nodes. This could be as bad as, or worse than, removing them. Whew! What a lucky escape she had.

With the Gerson Therapy the person would benefit from a massive re-alkalising, oxidation, and detoxification of their blood/body which would restore it to a state of balance. This highly oxidised and alkalised blood/body is incompatible with cancer growth and this would have been the reason Teresa Kay got rid of her cancer and survived.

If allopathic practitioners are sincere about cancer cure, shouldn't they exhaustively investigate all possibilities? Why don't they give the principles espoused in the Gerson Therapy a clinical trial and tell us the result? Is it because they couldn't make any money from this? My research tells me that they are not interested in trying anything that is not made in a laboratory and patentable. What do you think?

So, after the two revealing clinical trials – the Warburg experiment in 1924, plus the Cancer Research UK 2009 Oxygen therapy, what are they still researching? How many questions do they need answers to in order to solve the problem of cancer? Well, let's apply common sense and science to it, and see if they need to do any more research. Question one: what causes cells to become cancerous? Dr. Warburg has already established that it is an acidic blood and, as a consequence, a low level of oxygen-flow. The 2009 clinical trial confirmed it. Are they researching how to reverse the process that leads to cancer? The 2009 clinical trial (in particular) gave them more than a hint of how this can be done by demonstrating how cancer cells respond to oxygen.

Secondly, fermentation, which causes the body to become more acidic and is integral to the metastasis (spreading) of cancer, only becomes an issue *after* the cells have been starved of oxygen. Thirdly, the principle of having a slightly alkaline pH balance and its relationship to good health is already well established. So, to repeat, what are they still researching regarding the nature of and solution for cancer? Are they searching for a drug that is going to magically oxygenate the body's cells, reverse the body from its unhealthy acidic pH balance to an alkaline one, and detoxify the body? No drug or herb can do all of this.

There is absolutely no reason why the above principles cannot be applied to provide the solution for the cancer epidemic. Why hasn't it been done? Because the above principles are outside of their remit. They are driven by the pharmaceutical industry which is stuck in a drug paradigm solution, and this is self-evident by their reaction to the results of both clinical trials. The results from both trials were deemed by them to require a drugs solution, which is not surprising since they are in the drugs-to-cure-disease business. The problem is, their conclusion is not helping us.

The Teresa Kay story demonstrates that the body can revert to its healthy state after cancer as severe as lymphoma.

THE AMAZING LYMPHATIC SYSTEM

HAIL TO FRUITS AND VEGETABLES

Consider the following scenario: one aspect of your defence system which is able to protect you against cancer has itself become cancerous. Do you need to be a doctor or scientist to recognise the difficulty of overcoming cancer that had spread throughout such an area? One of the critical jobs of the lymphatic system is to provide the means by which waste products (poisons) like carbon dioxide (CO_2) can flow out of the cells and into lymph fluid. The lymph fluid filters the carbon dioxide into the blood stream, and the blood would move it to, and ultimately expel it through the lungs. Carbon dioxide being used, or fed upon by cancer cells, is said to be a major factor in the spreading (metastasis) of cancer. So having your lymphatic system compromised with cancer is the equivalent of going to your doctor for treatment and discovering that he/she is also helplessly sick.

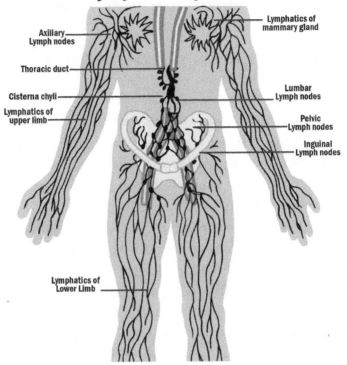

Lymphatic System

Look at the diagram above, which depicts the extensive network of the lymphatic system. If cancer were to spread within this lymphatic system, it would be very hard to treat it using conventional chemotherapy. Yet Teresa Kay did not use what we customarily define as 'medicine' and she is still alive today.

The question is: if allopathic medicine's best effort (chemotherapy) has been struggling for nearly seventy years to deal with the cancer problem, and this treatment causes innumerable damage to the body, how highly should we rate the alternative power of raw vegetables and fruits? These products of Nature got rid of Theresa's cancer, and caused no damage. Could her lymphoma be gotten rid of by what might have been considered a fluke? Nature does not operate flukes. Nature operates on a precise science of cause and effect.

Should we not study and learn from the Teresa Kay example? Are we so arrogant to think that we know more than Nature? Are we so arrogant to think that it is only through our manipulations of Nature, via the production of chemicals and synthetic drugs, often using natural raw materials, that Nature can help us? When are we going to drop this arrogance and give deference to Nature? Do we need to understand in every detail how Nature performs its miracles, or should we just say, 'Hail to fruits and vegetables?'

In the introduction, I quoted the World Health Organisation (WHO) as saying that low fruit and vegetable intake is one of the five leading factors that contribute to 30% of cancer deaths. I also pointed out that this is the same as saying fruits and vegetables can protect the body against cancer. Well, if they can protect us against cancer, why wouldn't they be able to help us overcome cancer?

In a state of illness as severe and as life threatening as cancer, the pancreas, which produces digestive enzymes, may fail to function at its optimum. In such a case the body would benefit enormously from foods rich in enzymes and nutrients that it can use *easily* for energy. I refer to the pancreas for a very important reason. It is a major organ which helps the body to digest foods. It plays an essential role in converting the food we eat into fuel for the body's cells. The pancreas has two main functions: an **exocrine** function that helps in digestion and an **endocrine** function that regulates blood sugar. This latter function regulates blood sugar and protects us against diabetes.

Maintaining proper *blood sugar levels* is crucial to the functioning of key organs, including the brain, liver, and kidneys. Cancer-treating drugs used in chemotherapy can damage the pancreas and therefore restrict its ability to perform these vital, life maintaining functions.

By avoiding these chemotherapy chemicals and giving her body a massive infusion of life-giving nutrients, Teresa Kay's immune system, very capable of defending her body, was aided by the live energy and *oxygen* that comes from raw foods. The immune system I'm referring to is not restricted to the blood (platelets) that attack germs. The immune system is also a term that loosely refers to the actions of the already mentioned lymphatic system, the pancreas, the liver, the kidneys and the adrenal glands. The pancreas produces the hormone insulin to obtain energy from glucose-sugar and this energy is essential for the healthy functioning of the body. If constantly stressed by drugs used in chemotherapy, it would eventually weaken and collapse. *The pancreas is not known to be very resilient; therefore, it has very limited powers of recovery if it is damaged.*

By avoiding the harsh chemotherapy drugs, Teresa also protected her kidneys. Our kidneys help us deal with toxins – such as drugs, which it tries to dilute through the production of urine. If constantly stressed by toxins the kidney deteriorates and loses its ability to dilute. Unlike the millions who die even after receiving chemotherapy drugs, Teresa Kay benefitted from avoiding this treatment because she also helped protect her adrenal glands in addition to her kidneys.

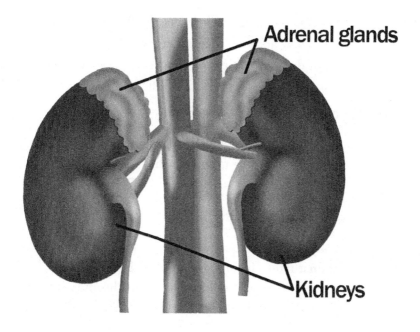

Adrenal glands

Kidneys

The adrenal glands are also part of the body's intelligent, defence system. These glands produce hormones such as adrenaline whenever the body is in a crisis. Healthy cells being destroyed by harsh chemo drugs would be treated as a crisis by the intelligent body! Adrenaline helps the body adjust to sudden stress by increasing the pulse (blood flow) and speeding up the conversion of food to energy. Some of this energy would be directed towards getting rid of the poisons (the chemo drugs) that are killing healthy cells of the body. However, whilst adrenaline is beneficial to the body in a crisis, having to respond continuously to the trauma of the chemo drugs constitutes an excessive demand of energy, and is injurious to the body.

In a cancer crisis *without* chemo drugs, the adrenal glands can help combat this situation. If the body is given the right nutrients to strengthen it, the adrenaline it releases has access to more 'fuel' to convert into energy which could help deal with mutated cancer cells. However, had Teresa allowed chemotherapy drugs/poisons into her system, it would demand a higher adrenaline output to combat this additional crisis. The crisis has now multiplied. In summary:

- there is the crisis of the cancer cells;

- there is the crisis of having a harsh, cell-killing drug in the body (which is killing unhealthy **and** healthy cells);

- there is the crisis of the body overtaxing its resources to constantly release adrenaline.

- the body being swamped with adrenaline is, in itself, harmful. It's not natural to be in a prolonged heightened state. Adrenaline is described as the 'flight or fright' hormone. In such a state, the body cannot be relaxed, and relaxation is a vital part of good health.

The adrenal glands do not have an unlimited supply of adrenalin. If Teresa had experienced prolonged use of chemotherapy, the adrenal glands would eventually not be able to keep up with the raised level of poisons in the body and the extreme stress. This means that the adrenal glands would lose their ability to deal with the combined crisis generated from the cancer and effects of chemo drugs/poisons. Any drug that kills the body's cells will be treated by the intelligent body as a crisis and it will stimulate the release of adrenaline.

Teresa Kay also avoided having her liver damaged by chemo drugs. The liver stores vitamins and minerals and supplies energy. Its primary job, however, is to deal with toxins. For example, it protects our body against the effects of toxins such as alcohol. Where alcohol is taken to excess, cirrhosis of the liver results, which is a hardening of the organ. Constant intake of any toxin, including chemo drugs, weakens the liver's ability to protect the body. All the organs involved with immunity have upper limits to their ability to perform their role. Teresa could have ended up with a cascading effect of one organ after another fighting for and then failing to maintain wellness; and eventually, wellness would have been lost as the organs, one by one, ceased to function optimally.

The medical system, as it is now, does not give nutrition a major role in the treatment of any major disease. It ignores the obvious fact that it is nutrients which keep us alive! We cannot eat and survive on drugs! Since nutrients keep us alive, why should they not play a part in helping us recover from illness? During major illness, the body needs the very best nutrition. In particular, it needs nutrients that can be easily absorbed and assimilated/digested. The body is best able to absorb and assimilate fruits, vegetables, and other plant nutrients that are uncooked.

They are far more easily digested than any cooked meal and, of critical importance, they have 'live' enzymes. This is what Dr. Dana Myatt has to say about enzymes: *Plant enzymes assist digestion, improve assimilation and help correct the chronic health problems.*

(http://www.drmyattswellnessclub.com/enzymes.htm)

Eating uncooked vegetables, fruits and nuts, add additional enzymes to the digestive system. Enzymes facilitate the production of energy for the body. This is the same as saying enzymes are critical in the preservation and extension of life. Listen to Dr Myatt again:

Life is a series of chemical reactions. These reactions would occur too slowly to support life without the aid of enzymes. Enzymes act as biochemical catalysts, "sparking" the chemical reactions that are the basis of all physical function.

Digestive enzymes are mainly made by the pancreas and are necessary for assimilation of nutrients from food. Without these enzymes, the body cannot absorb energy (calories) efficiently.

As stated above, chemotherapy drugs weaken the pancreas and the digestive system in general. This is why people lose their appetite during treatment, and why it can take up to six weeks to return to normal levels after the treatment ends. This means that the time during which the body especially needs nutrients that can build and repair it, becomes the time that the person's desire to eat it suppressed. The treatment is therefore incompatible with wellness. **Nutrients are the only physical things that promote wellness.**

It takes energy to digest food, so, in the weakened state of illness, the less energy we demand of the body to digest foods, the more energy the body has to defend itself and repair any damage. In effect, by eating foods that do not take a lot of effort/energy to digest, we give the system a rest, so that the body can more effectively do what is its main drive at that time: the countering of the illness.

Teresa Kay would have stopped eating all the foods and changed the lifestyle that had caused her body to become cancerous in the first place. If a person had lung cancer caused by smoking, no treatment would be effective if the person continued to smoke. This example epitomises the essential logic of reversing cancer: get rid of the underlying cause and then repair the damage.

In 1993, the National Cancer Institute published the result of a study with women who had been treated for breast cancer. They told half the women to continue with their typical American diet, and asked the other half to change to a plant based diet. After only four years, almost 40% of women who stayed on their animal based diet had recurrences of breast cancer. However, not a single woman who changed to a plant based diet had a recurrence of breast cancer. – Mike Anderson (The Rave Diet DVD Documentary)

Why is the above not general knowledge? Why has this not become the common approach within the cancer industry? Dr. Ruth Heidrich, who received her PhD in Health Management in 1993, is the author of "A Race for Life" and "The Race for Life Cookbook."

She is a certified fitness trainer and holds three world records for fitness for her age group at the renowned Cooper Clinic in Dallas, Texas. She still actively competes in marathons and triathlons, having won more than 800 trophies and medals since her diagnosis of breast cancer in 1982 at the age of 47. She developed cancer even though she was eating better and exercising more than government guidelines. Her initial reaction was that she was too 'healthy' to have cancer because she was a marathon runner at the time and she had a 'healthy' diet.

She had surgery to remove the tumour from her breast. After the surgery, she was faced with the prospect of chemotherapy and radiation treatments to kill cancer cells that had spread throughout her body. According to Dr. Heidrich: *When I was told that I needed chemotherapy and radiation, I was dreading it; it was scary; I really did not want poison injected in my veins. And having worked for the military, I knew what radiation damage could do to a body. I did not want that. So, I was looking for somebody, something, to tell me another way. I just intuitively felt that there has to be another answer.*

She sought five 'second opinions' until she found Dr. John McDougall, M.D. She was not eating at the time what she called 'the standard American diet', so she felt that her cancer was not due to her diet. According to Dr. Heidrich: *I 'knew' that it was not diet in my case because, I was not eating any red meat; I only had skim milk, and chicken and fish. When I went to see Dr. McDougall he said, "That's the diet that caused your breast cancer." I was shocked! He said, "If you want to save your life, change your diet." And of course my response was, let's prove it one way or the other. And then I thought, oh, it's too late. And he said, "No, it's not too late …you've removed the tumour; now what your body has to do is a mop up operation. And that is what diet enables your immune system to do.*" She went on to say, *Breast cancer is a symptom of a lousy diet.*

We see that she refused chemotherapy and radiation treatment and switched to a one hundred percent plant based diet. Now, thirty years later, she is cancer free and credits her new diet for saving her life. Three weeks after changing to a plant based diet, her cholesterol level dropped from 236 to 160. And cholesterol is a major factor in the cause of cancer.

EFFECT OF CHOLESTEROL ON OUR ARTERIES

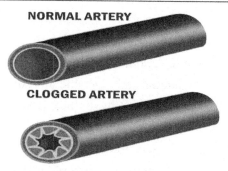

The outer circle is the natural circumference of the artery. The narrow 'circle' is a result of the build-up of cholesterol. This reduces the volume of blood which will flow through the artery per unit time, which will also reduce the supply of oxygen to our cells. This reduction of oxygen supply to cells is the cornerstone of many diseases, including cancer. Do not be confused by those who will point out that the body produces cholesterol and therefore animal cholesterol is not harmful. Everything that a healthy body produces is in aid of sustaining life and this includes its *own cholesterol.* Our body is no more compatible with using another animal's cholesterol than it is with using another animal's organs, or blood. Furthermore, our liver produces all the cholesterol we will ever need. As mammals we are compatible with our *own mother's* milk, however, we are not compatible with another animal's milk. Nor should other animals be raised on our milk. It would not help them to thrive in the way they are meant to thrive.

If most people ate large amounts of raw fruits and vegetables as part of their daily diet, and fewer animal products, the global proliferation of disease would not be what it is today. – Author

Prevention is better than cure – wise proverb

WHAT IS THE CORRECT HUMAN DIET?

It seem to me that the popularly accepted definition of our dietary type is that we are omnivores. An omnivore is defined as an animal that can naturally feed on both animal and vegetable substances. This is the definition that most people accept. Why do most people accept that we are omnivores? I believe that it is accepted because this is the current dietary practice of most human beings. In effect, this is the only reality of which we are aware. Therefore, we tend to regard vegetarianism as some sort of fad, oddity, extremism, or those who adopt this diet may be called, to use the common oxymoron, a 'health freak'. The fact that people would regard a person to be a freak because they appear to be overly concerned about their health tells its own story.

It speaks of a situation where people are so programmed to eat for entertainment, taste, or pleasure, that the idea that we are to eat primarily in order to sustain our lives in a state of good health, is now an oddity at best, or freakish at worse. As far as I am aware, human beings are the only creatures on this planet who eat primarily for taste, where health is a secondary consideration. This is because we have the power of choice. All other life-forms are programmed to eat for survival.

I take the view that we are herbivores. This means that we are supposed to feed solely on plant matter. The fact that we eat both meat and vegetables is no more proof that we are meant to be omnivores than the fact that we smoke proves that we are *supposed to* ingest smoke. Eating meat, drinking alcohol, or smoking merely demonstrates that we can force our bodies to accept any substance that does not have a level of toxicity that would cause immediate death. The body will accept poison in small doses. My reasons for concluding that we are only supposed to eat plant foods are varied. However, here are the primary ones:

- The way we are designed is like other vegetarian animals. Vegetarian animals have relatively long intestines. Omnivorous animals have much shorter intestines. We can look at the chimpanzee, for example; it is classified as an omnivore, as it eats both plant and animal materials. If you compare it with an orang-utan (also a member of the ape family) which primarily eats fruits, but only eats lower quality foods, such as bark, leaves and termites, in times of scarcity, you will see that its intestines are more than twice the length of the chimpanzee's, even though it is a smaller animal.

- Carnivores have greatly enlarged stomachs which encompass between 60 and 70 percent of their entire digestive tracts, while herbivores have much smaller stomachs as they generally are required to process smaller amounts of food.

- The kidneys of carnivores and omnivores create extremely concentrated urine, again differing from the kidneys of herbivores which produce weakly concentrated urine

- We chew our foods just like vegetarian and fruitarian animals. We chew our food in a sort of circular motion, repeatedly, and roll it into a 'ball' before we swallow it. This is the first part of our digestive process. Natural meat eaters do not chew their food. They cut and swallow. They chomp up, and down with minimal sideways motion. Some of us appear to try to imitate these animals, and what did our parents tell us? Take your time and chew your food!

- Herbivores and omnivores have enzymes in their saliva to aid with the breakdown of *plant matter: carbohydrates*. However, omnivores do not practice repetitive chewing, as do herbivores. In the case of carnivorous animals, they do not have such enzymes.

- Our digestion starts in our mouth with our saliva. Saliva contains a digestive enzyme which is alkaline and used for the digestion of carbohydrates and natural sugars. These are derived from plant materials.

- The fact that we practice repetitive chewing, even when we eat meat, proves that *we are not natural meat eaters* because repetitive chewing releases the enzyme ptyalin which only digests carbohydrates/natural sugars but does not break down meat (protein).

- Repetitive chewing and having a carbohydrate digesting enzyme within saliva indic*ates that carbohydrate digestio*n is intended to start in the mouth, demonstrating that the animal is an herbivore.

- Any animal that does not practice repetitive chewing is designed to eat meat/protein alone, because the stomach is where enzymes exist to digest meat/protein. An enzyme which breaks down protein would damage the inside of the animal's mouth because it is very acidic. This is why carnivores don't chew, but swallow their food (meat) in whole chunks.

- Natural meat eaters (carnivores and omnivores) are well adapted to eat raw meat. They are also capable of digesting the hair from the animal. We cannot eat raw meat extensively without developing illnesses. We are also not capable of digesting hair.

- A carnivore's teeth are long, sharp and pointed. Some omnivore's have teeth which are similar to that of carnivores. Human, as well as other herbivore's teeth are not pointed but flat edged. These are useful tools for biting, crushing and the grinding of grains and nuts. Do not misinterpret the significance of the fact that humans have canines. They are very inadequate for tearing raw meat; therefore, they are not comparable to those of certain omnivorous or carnivorous animals.

- Carnivorous animals swallow their food (meat) whole and/or only with simple crushing.

- A carnivore's stomach secretes powerful digestive enzymes which have about ten times more hydrochloric acid than a human or other herbivore. This powerful acid enables it to destroy things such as E. coli bacteria, salmonella, trichina worms (parasites), or other pathogens found in meat. These things will not survive in the stomach of a lion or tiger, etc.

- That we are not designed to be carnivorous is evident by the fact that many carnivores can secrete digestive acids powerful enough to dissolve and digest bone. We are incapable of this feat. The pH balance in the stomach of a carnivore can be 1 or less than 1 with food in the stomach. The acidity of our stomach can only range from 4 to 5 with food in it.

- The evidence is overwhelming that meat is the sole source of LDL cholesterol (low-density lipoprotein cholesterol), and LDL cholesterol is the harmful cholesterol that is known to cause death among us. The most commonly known cause of death among us is heart disease, which is primarily caused by the LDL cholesterol from meat. This proves that we are not natural meat eaters. Cholesterol does not cause illness in naturally meat-eating animals, even though they eat their meat raw.

For example, *lions and tigers, who are natural meat eaters, do not experience heart disease.*

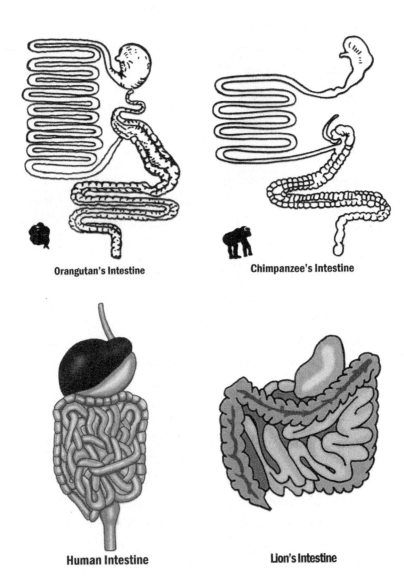

Orangutan's Intestine

Chimpanzee's Intestine

Human Intestine

Lion's Intestine

- As can be seen by the diagrams, our intestines are comparatively longer than an animal that periodically eats meat, such as the chimpanzee. It is also twice as long as a carnivore's, such as a lion. These animals' intestine is 3 to 6 times the length of their trunk. An herbivore's small intestine, however, is 10 to 12 times the length of its trunk, and winds itself back and forth in random directions. This is designed for keeping food in it for long enough periods of time to extract all the valuable nutrients and minerals before the food enters the large intestine. This fits the description of our intestine.

- Our intestines are more in line with the orang-utan's, whose primary diet is fruit. The benefit for the meat-eating animal of having a short intestine is that it allows the meat to leave the body in a short period of time. This is important because meat by its nature has toxins in it, such as adrenaline, which the animal releases upon being killed. Our intestine is long, and therefore does not facilitate the quick elimination of meat. This means that meat will stay in the body too long, and this can be up to 72 hours – by this time the body starts to absorb the gasses and toxins produced by the meat. Also, the relatively short intestine of a carnivore or omnivore enables it to easily eliminate fatty wastes high in cholesterol before they start to putrefy.

The human body maintains good health with a slightly alkaline pH balance (see chapter 1, page 48). The vast majority of fruits and vegetables are alkaline-forming foods. The same cannot be said for virtually all animal-based foods. They are virtually all acid-forming foods or carry the unhealthy baggage of cholesterol. Within these realities also lays the truth as to what the correct human diet is supposed to be...herbal/vegetable-based foods.

You've read where researchers who published The Rave Diet declared that:

Before the nineteen hundreds, heart disease, our biggest killer, wasn't even included in medical text books. And cancer, diabetes, arthritis, and our other major diseases were rare, and confined to the wealthy, who ate like most Americans eat today.

I call this 'the science of observation'. If certain activities consistently are associated with certain consequences, it is a simple deduction to conclude that the results are related to the activities. The problem is that most of us are unaware of the connection between what we eat and the illness we experience. This produces a paradigm that gives birth to a word that should become the most feared. The word that we should become afraid of is the simple word 'normal'. Why should we be afraid of this word? Without the perspective of history, everything that is widely practiced, or that which is a common outcome, will be seen as normal. This is why there is no international panic regarding the millions of deaths from diseases among young people, and people well below a hundred years old. In contrast to this, we always have a panic when any form of abnormality appears among animals, domestic animals in particular. In recent years we've seen great panic caused by the outbreak of 'mad cow' disease and the resurgence of 'foot and mouth' disease in the UK.

The acceptance of what is normal also applies to the pharmaceutical industry. From the medical and the pharmaceutical industry we have learnt to accept that it is normal to take synthetic drugs as medicines. Yet, for most of human medical history the world practiced naturopathic medicine or herbal medicine. This type of medicine by nature doesn't have side effects; which means, it doesn't harm the body unless we overdose. From this, you should understand that the term 'side effect', as applied to allopathic medicine, means that the 'medicine' has harmed your body, even when we don't overdose. So now you have an additional problem. You now need another 'medicine' to deal with the side effect!

Even now, the dominant medicine is not allopathic or chemical medicine. China, one of the most populous nations, still uses herbal medicine in their hospitals. I saw this on my visit there. Herbal medicine is still widely used in another populous nation, India. This is also true, but to lesser extent on the continents of Africa and Asia, and the regions of the Caribbean and Central America.

Hurdles to overcome

THE LIMITATIONS OF GOVERNMENT IN SOLVING THE CANCER PROBLEM

- Governments are made up of people whose general attitudes are not vastly different from the rest of us.

- Members of Parliament (or Congress) have political and economic biases that are likely to affect their desire to go on a crusade against companies that sell foods that are harmful (junk food).

- Therefore, governments need to be influenced by a groundswell of public opinion that is generated by an exposure to the truths surrounding cancer. I hope this book will play a part in causing such a groundswell.

Governments need to go through a transformation in their attitude to drugs companies in the same way they changed their attitude towards cigarette companies. There is now a general, concerted effort to stop people from smoking. Prior to this it seems that governments primarily saw the tobacco industry as a 'cash-cow'. Come budget time, it seemed as if they used it as an easy source of raising revenue. I now assume that they have done the maths and recognise that they were/are losing more than they are gaining. Perhaps they did a tally of the cost of the loss of lives to the economy (the brain drain factor) and the cost of medical care of cigarette smoking sufferers, and those who suffer as a result of passive smoking. This cost would be significantly greater than revenue gained through taxation on tobacco.

The revenue gained from the cancer research industry will be minuscule compared to the cost of lives that is the result of the inability to solve this major illness. Furthermore, if the cancer research industry is transformed, or replaced by an industry that provides more effective treatments, there still would be a revenue stream for governments. This principle also applies to switching from a meat intensive economy to a fruit and vegetable intensive economy. Animals and the earth's resources would breathe a collective sigh of relief if this became a reality.

The challenge to shift to a culture of healthy eating is one of gigantic proportions. It is almost an intractable problem because it is driven by the most powerful factor there is: demand. Once people become accustomed to eating certain foods, and since these foods are usually very addictive, the demand dictates their production. Governments are also restricted by the fact that in democratic countries people don't want a 'nanny state'. Many people hold the view that governments should not interfere with their personal or private choices, such as what they should eat or drink. This attitude is demonstrated by some people campaigning for the legalisation of illicit drugs.

Even with something as obviously detrimental as cigarettes and alcohol, governments are limited to warnings and advertising restrictions. Furthermore, prohibitions don't work to stop people from consuming harmful things in the way education would. Education is most effective in helping people to act in their best self-interest when it comes to decisions and practices regarding harmful foods and other harmful substances. Educating the public more is one of the roles governments should play. The other should be the enactment of legislation to enable a more even playing field for natural therapies to compete where the drugs companies dominate.

The nature of the cancer disease points to a non-chemical solution. However, if the system in place is locked into a paradigm of a drug solution, then there will be no solution. The drug solution practice has continuously grown, and even though it is accepted by the World Health Organisation (WHO) and some others within the medical fraternity that diet is related to disease, the science of medicine and the science of food still exists in parallel universes. This is because they still have not credited food as the solution. So, even though the World Health Organisation acknowledges the link between diet and cancer, there has been no *concerted effort* equal to the severity of the problem to highlight the foods that cause cancer. If eating certain foods cause cancer, does it not makes sense to stop eating them as part of the cure?

On the one hand, the allopathic medicine world has grown into a massive multi-trillion dollar monster that is riddled with self-interest. On the other hand, the food industry has grown into an even bigger monster that is riddled with even more self-interest. Therefore, even though it is established in small circles that meat causes cancer, this message will struggle to get into the mainstream.

A reasonable alternative to focusing on diseases and the suppressing of their symptoms with drugs, would be to focus on wholeness; on health, and on only giving the body something that will immediately improve its healing capabilities. Naturally high energy nutrients support the immune system and the body's natural healing powers. In a diseased state the body's resistance is already run down; so we should only introduce substances and nutrients which will have a direct healing and immune-enhancing effect.

It is a little known fact that medical doctors have very little knowledge about nutrition. This is true because medical schools offer little or no education on nutrition, vitamins or minerals. This is verified by Dr. Ray Strand, the author of *Death by Prescription*, who stated:

In medical school I had not received any significant instruction on the subject. I was not alone. Only approximately 6 percent of the graduating physicians in the United States have any training in nutrition. Medical students may take elective courses on the topic, but few actually do... the education of most physicians is disease-oriented with a heavy emphasis on pharmaceuticals — we learn about drugs and why and when to use them.

To be honest, I knew next to nothing about nutrition or nutritional supplementation.... Because of the respect people have for doctors, they assume we are experts on all health-related issues, including nutrition and vitamins. Before my conversion experience with nutritional medicine, my patients frequently asked me if I believed their taking vitamins produced any health benefits.... Handing the bottles back, I'd say that the stuff was absolutely no use at all.... What I did not share with my patients was that I had not spent a minute evaluating the hundreds of scientifically conducted studies that proved the value of supplementation to health.

For the first twenty-three years of my clinical practice, I simply did not believe in nutritional supplements. During the past seven years, however, I have reconsidered my position based on recent studies published in the medical literature. What I've found is so astonishing, I have changed the course of my medical practice...

Physicians seem content to allow the pharmaceutical companies to determine new therapies as they develop new drugs... physicians are simply too busy treating disease to worry about educating their patients in healthy lifestyles that help avoid developing degenerative diseases in the first place. As I have applied these principles in treating my patients the results have been nothing short of amazing. (http://goo.gl/34e1z)

To change the system even moderately, the above medical curriculum that Dr. Strand mentioned has to change. – Author

---

Food and Drug industries have an enormous influence on the curriculum that medical and agricultural colleges set. This influence is obvious in respect to the drug companies, since they are the ones who research and develop the drugs that doctors recommend to their patients. This is not the ideal. It would be better if the colleges set the basis on which treatments should be developed. A curriculum that is influenced by drug companies would be tainted by self-interest. If curricula are set by the colleges based on wellness principles without any influence from drug companies, then such courses would not possibly have information that would help drug companies with their profit consideration. This would be the ideal.

If the colleges that have relationships with drug companies were operated strictly on an academic basis and were not allowed to have financial incentives that could constitute a conflict of interest, their sole concern would be the welfare of people. Therefore, they would not satisfy the self-interest of their teachers or any drug company. The interest of the drugs companies is unavoidably tainted by the self-interest to sell drugs, make a profit and stay in business. The self-interest is compounded by a major characteristic of business, which is to expand market share. This is incompatible with what the colleges' teaching objective should be. The following information should, at minimum, highlight the fact that close relationships between learning institutions and commercial enterprises cause conflicts of interest:

The New York Times printed an article on June 8, 2008 under the heading: *Researchers fail to reveal full drug pay*. The article stated:

A renowned Harvard child psychiatrist whose work has helped fuel an explosion in the use of powerful antipsychotic medicines in children earned at least $1.6 million in consulting fees from drug makers from 2000 to 2007, but for years did not report much of this income to university officials, according to information given to Congressional investigators.

By failing to report this income, the psychiatrist, Dr.... and a colleague in the psychiatry department at Harvard Medical School, Dr.... may have violated federal and university rules designed to police potential conflicts of interest, according to Senator Charles E. Grassley, Republican of Iowa.

The above serves to highlight the intractable nature of the conflict between personal incentive and public interest inherent in the promotion of allopathic medicine, replete with its side effects.

BODY SCIENCE VS. FOOD SCIENCE

HOW TO CHANGE YOUR DIET

The absence of a divine dietary instruction manual has placed the onus on us to learn about our body and its care. – Author

As I've already stated, changing our dietary culture is a challenge of gigantic proportions. This is because the most popular foods are, generally speaking, very addictive. Once we develop a liking for certain foods, it becomes ingrained in our pleasure centre, and therefore a source of enjoyment. We become attached to these foods, and since life is about enjoyment, it takes an incredible shift in mindset to change and to wean ourselves from foods that are *made* to taste good with additives and chemicals.

We now have a situation where there are cultures who have converted eating into a vice by adding chemicals to our foods, which should only be regarded as immoral. The 'food' industry is so highly competitive that it has invented a situation where there is intense creativity in applying dangerous additives and preservatives in the manufacturing of more tasty 'new foods', sauces, etc. The addition of these chemicals makes such 'food' taste 'good' and highly addictive, which therefore will foster regular consumption to 'entertain our taste buds'. This creativity extends to the ways in which meals are prepared, and is regarded by many as imaginative cooking. Celebrity chefs and chefs in expensive restaurants are particularly known for this type of cooking. You may find the following quote of interest:

In a survey of cookbook and television recipes by celebrity chefs released last month, the **University of Coventry** *found that 87% failed to meet the minimum national health standards. The study, carried out in Britain... argued that the superchef recipes extolled fatty, artery-clogging ingredients such as bacon and butter to pump up flavors.*

(http://www.thebraiser.com/study-celebrity-chefs-call-unhealthy-food-study-bs/)

In the quest for a healthy longevity, we have to learn to eat to live, instead of living to eat. – Author

---

This general 'eating as entertainment' also includes snacking. The snack food industry has fuelled the growth of this habit. This industry is a monster in the arena of producing unhealthy 'foods'. What is even worse is that this industry promotes nonstop eating; which means eating even when we are not hungry. A further, deadly factor which has turned eating into a vice is the addition of salt and sugar into our foods. These two non-foods are preservatives and are very addictive. Giving up salt was the thing I found most difficult to do. I suspect that salty food is just as addictive as illegal drugs.

I know it's easier to change one's diet gradually, because this was my experience. These are the things I found easy to do:

- I found it easy to eat fruit first thing in the morning, once I found out that fruits are best eaten on an empty stomach. This is when they don't cause wind to develop in the system.

- It was easy to switch from white flour to whole-meal flour. Some people may find it easier to start by mixing whole-meal flour with the white flour they are more used to.

- It was easy for me to give up sugar. I could satisfy any taste for sweetness using fruits. Furthermore, I didn't think I would look that good without my teeth, if they are decayed by sugar. Secondly, I had extra motivation after contemplating the suggestion that if sugar can rot bones, what might it do to the soft tissues of one's body?

- Giving up salt was initially very difficult. However, it became easier once I discovered that adding a bit of cayenne pepper to the meal was an adequate replacement.

- Before I finally gave up meat I switched to using cold-pressed oil to cook it, or to fry foods. This type of oil is produced without the use of any heat; therefore, when used to cook, it would be the first time it is heated. With other types of oils, cooking is the second time the oil is being heated. The science of this is that each time the oil is heated, it becomes more complex and therefore harder for the body to break down. This is a major contribution to the unhealthy nature of fast and fried foods, and is particularly true in the making of potato chips (fries) and chicken. They are repeatedly fried in the same oil. I find it interesting that cold-pressed oils are not widely available to the common consumer, and are mostly sold in health shops. It's also interesting that in any given area we will find hundreds of food shops, yet very few are called *health food* shops.

- Once I found out about the unhealthy nature of fried foods and the heating of oils, I stopped using oil as a part of the cooking process. I instead used the juice from tomatoes and whatever fat that is within the meat itself. So, I basically stewed everything, and guess what? The food didn't lose any of its taste!

- I discovered that the combination of protein and carbohydrate in the same meal was the reason for drowsiness after eating. If eating induces tiredness, it is not a good practice. It was therefore easy for me to stop this unhealthy, energy sapping practice. It was a simple case of switching to eating meats with vegetables, and eating carbohydrates with vegetables. You will never experience drowsiness after eating in this way. I would suggest you read about *Food Combining* for more information on the subject.

- It was easy for me to give up the unhealthy habit of eating and drinking at the same time. Drinking while eating dilutes and disrupts the digestive process. For example, the digestion of carbohydrates involves chewing it into a 'ball' before swallowing. The digestive enzyme ptyalin provided by the saliva, would be enmeshed in the 'ball', and requires time to breakdown/digest the carbohydrate. Adding liquid during this process will disperse the 'ball', and therefore, at minimum, prolong the digestive process, and at worse, cause carbohydrates to be undigested. The ingestion of any liquid is recommended to be before eating, or an hour after eating. We are the only living beings who eat and drink at the same time. For example, you will never see a lion have a drink between swallowing chunks of an antelope's leg.

- Once I understood the unhealthy nature of meat, I gradually reduced my intake until I could switch to only fish. If I knew then what I know now, I would have switched to meat substitutes instead of fish. I gradually switched to meat substitutes, and I eventually became a vegan.

All of the above, unreformed, eating habits are bad individually. However, all of them combined can be lethal. Be mindful of this definition of failure: a few errors in judgment practiced every day.

CHAPTER FOUR

SOME FOODS AND LIFESTYLE RELATIONSHIP TO CANCER AND DISEASES

The more acidic the blood is, the less oxygen it contains, and the faster a person ages and degenerates. On a practical level, this means we should do everything to keep the pH on the high side of the range, as close as possible to 7.45, by eating as many alkaline foods as possible. That would be, you guessed it – live, raw foods, especially green foods. –Dr Tim O'Shea

I sometimes reflect on some of the common, ignorant philosophies I have heard about our bodies throughout my formative years, much of which are still embraced today. One such philosophy states: "If your stomach is receptive to a 'food', it can be eaten." The idea that each item we ingest into our system has its own scientific characteristics, and that this science needs to be compatible with the body's scientific characteristics, will be strange to those who have not considered this reality. Vomiting and heartburn are two examples of the body's 'science of incompatibility'. Vomiting is a demonstration that our body is intelligent and will take action to preserve its health.

You've read that a tumour is the intelligent body's way of protecting its life by removing the cancer cells from general circulation within the body. If you accept that the body is intelligent, you should accept that the body will react intelligently to any substance that we put in it. The following 'food' items demonstrate that it is dangerous to accept the philosophy that states, 'if your stomach accepts a 'food' or drink, it can 'absorb' it', therefore making it acceptable to consume such items. Here are examples of how the body reacts to some 'foods', drink, and tobacco smoke – both legal and illegal:

BLEACHED WHITE FLOUR, WHITE RICE, ETC.

Bleached white flour is wholemeal flour that has been stripped of its vital nutrients. At minimum, the body would not find this substance to be very useful, because it is designed to process nutrients. This is why such foods are referred to by naturopaths as *starvation foods*. These 'foods' starve the body of nutrients and oxygen. Consumption of an excess of this type of 'food' can lead to being overfed but undernourished. This type of 'food' is said to demand more oxygen to produce energy than do whole foods with their nutrients intact. Other 'foods' that are said to be major oxygen users are processed sugars, French fries, pizzas, and junk foods in general. These 'foods' deplete our 'oxygen store'. Any foods that deplete our oxygen stores will make us more prone to developing cancer.

The World Health Organisation mentions that a high body mass index increases the risk of cancer. This refers to being overweight or obese. An overweight or obese person will tend also to have excess cholesterol that clogs their arteries and veins. As already explained, this reduces the flow of blood and oxygen. The simple explanation of these 'foods' relationship to cancer is the same as the basic theme of this book: anything that reduces oxygen supply to cells can cause cancer.

FRIED FOODS

Fried foods often contain saturated fats. Such fats tend to increase bad cholesterol levels in our blood. Increased bad cholesterol levels in our blood will transform it to sludge, and blood in such a state will restrict the amount of oxygen going to our cells. This restriction of oxygen to our cells, not only cause cancer, but it is also known to be the principal reason why people suffer from strokes.

SALT

Salt causes high blood pressure. This strain upon the system can lead to eventual damage to our kidneys. If our kidneys are damaged, their ability to filter out unwanted and toxic waste products is reduced, so these products start to build up in the body. Since our kidneys are part of our defence system against cancer and other diseases, any substance that damages our kidneys can contribute to developing cancer. A build up of toxic waste in our body will certainly damage our cells, and damaged cells are often the trigger for developing cancer.

SUGARS

Consuming isolated and concentrated sugars raises insulin levels in the bloodstream, disrupting the blood-sugar balance within the body. Higher insulin levels will inhibit the release of growth hormones, which in turn depresses our immune system. This is because our system does not like isolated, concentrated, sugars. They affect our immune system because they can weaken and/or destroy our pancreas, liver and kidneys. With all that's already been said about the importance of these organs in defending us against diseases, you should now understand how the situations above and below can contribute to developing cancer.

Refined dietary sugars also qualify as starvation 'foods' because they lack minerals and vitamins of their own. In order to be metabolized/digested into the body's system, glucose must draw upon the body's own micro-nutrient stores. The body's micro-nutrients (vitamins/minerals) are stored in the liver. Therefore, when you eat concentrated sugars, you're robbing your liver to feed your body. The intelligent body cannot metabolize/digest sugars without them having minerals and vitamins that you would get from eating natural sugar in an apple, or orange, etc. Eating fruits is the only 'safe' way to eat sugar.

The American Dietetic Association and American Diabetic Association acknowledge that isolated, concentrated sugars are devoid of minerals, vitamins or fibre, and therefore have a deteriorating effect on the endocrine system (pancreas).

These organisations and researchers agree that sugar consumption in America is one of the major causes of degenerative disease. You should also consider this question: if sugar is powerful enough to rot our teeth which are made up of three of the hardest tissues in our body, what will it do to the soft tissues of our body?

ALCOHOL

Cancer Research UK states: *There is no doubt that alcohol can cause seven types of cancer.* They refer to cancer that shows up in the mouth, pharyngeal (back of throat), oesophageal (food pipe), laryngeal (voice box), breast, bowel, and the liver. The alcohol referred to is that within beers, wines, or liquors (distilled spirits). They all contain ethanol. How does alcohol cause cancer? The interesting thing about alcohol is that it acts on our body in a similar way to chemo drugs. It kills body cells. However, its effect is far milder than chemo drugs. Therefore, it damages or kills our cells through prolonged usage, and the rate of damage is affected by the strength and frequency of use. Alcohol is not a food, it is a drug.

The death of cells is a normal occurrence in the body, but in the normal course of events the body replaces these cells. However, in the case of the liver, if it loses its ability to deal with alcohol as a drug, we get cirrhosis of the liver, which is a hardening of the liver. Any substance that reduces the liver's ability to defend the body will make us more prone to cancer. Like alcohol, chemotherapy drugs reduce the liver's ability to defend the body. Another specific way that alcohol causes cancer is that it damages cells and therefore reduces their ability to utilise oxygen. And as been repeatedly stated, cells that are starved of oxygen can mutate and become cancerous. Alcohol is listed by the World Health Organisation as one of the major causes of cancer. So, let's take a further look at the effect it has on the liver in particular:

The liver is the largest gland in the body, and plays a major role in defending us against diseases. One of its many functions is to process and remove any alcohol, toxins or drugs. The liver is said to be very tough, and will continue working even after it is badly damaged. It can continue to repair itself until it is severely damaged. Yet, alcohol, one of the substances it is responsible for removing, is so powerful that it can almost literally 'fry' our liver and cause death. The disfigured liver below has the characteristic of being burnt, similarly to my experience of cooking or frying an animal's liver. This is called cirrhosis of the liver. Cirrhosis progresses slowly, over many years, gradually causing your liver to stop functioning. This is called liver failure. Here is a synopsis of the damage that alcohol causes to the liver and other organs:

- Causes the liver to become inflamed – hepatitis.

- Caused the liver to become hard – cirrhosis.

- Causes liver to lose its ability to produce digestive enzymes, neutralize toxins, store energy and absorb fats and proteins.

- Damages cells, tissues, nerves, organs and bones.

- Kills brain cells.

- Causes birth defects due to damages done to both men and women. This is because prolonged use of alcohol will damage sperms and eggs.

- In general, alcohol consumption in the form of beer, wine, and whiskey is anti-health and anti-life.

All of the above should strengthen your acceptance of the role alcohol can play in causing cancer.

Have a look at the before and after of cirrhosis of the liver below:

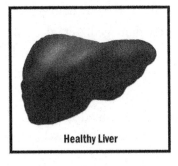
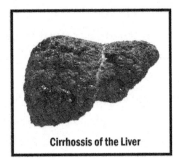

Healthy Liver

Cirrhossis of the Liver

Do you accept that any substance that can do this to the liver can also cause cancer?

SMOKING

The harm from smoking shouldn't require a lot of explanation. This is because it should be obvious that the body cannot utilize smoke. The body gets its nutrients from solids, liquids and one gas: oxygen. Even if a substance has nutritional or medical properties, the body cannot extract it through smoking. Once you burn a substance it becomes a drug.

Smoking produces carbon dioxide and tar, both of which are poisonous to our body. They clog up the lungs and therefore restrict the lung's capacity for oxygen. Smoking can cause cancer, and smoking also restricts oxygen supply. Here again oxygen is the centre of the cancer question.

STRESS

Many of us live very stressful lives. For whatever reason that we are stressed, it is still important to understand how stress can affect our health. We have all observed that when a person is frightened, blood drains from their face, and they are referred to as being 'ashen faced'. In effect, stress reduces blood and oxygen supply to the skin. It also reduces blood and oxygen to other vital organs such as the reproductive system, digestive system, and immune system. Therefore, a constantly stressful body can be a trigger for the causation of cancer. If our vital organs, such as those that comprise our immune system, are weakened by an inadequate supply of blood and oxygen, then a person can become prone to developing cancer. This is especially true if such a person also has a highly acidic diet caused by animal foods. These factors, combined with smoking; environmental and food chemicals; poor air quality; inadequate exercise; inadequate, or no fruit and vegetables intake; inadequate sleep to regenerate our cells to get back their vitality, etc. are factors that contribute to cancer being endemic in society today.

CONCLUSIONS

I would have called the naturopathic approach versus the drugs approach a 'war', aimed at capturing our attention, but this would be inappropriate. In our western culture, the drugs approach is so dominant and loud that the majority of us can hear nothing else. –Author

Because of the enormity of this problem, it is impossible for there not to be other viewpoints which contradict what I've presented. Established, unhealthy lifestyle practices are a contradiction of the many congruent viewpoints on healthy living that I've presented. Yet regardless of the contrasting viewpoints in relation to the cause of or character of cancer, the one thing that ought to stand out is that chemotherapy and radiotherapy treatments are not the way to solve this problem.

Self-interest dominates the medical industry. Self-interest is an inevitable human characteristic. However, there is a point at which self-interest can become insidious. This is where self-interest is achieved at any cost without consideration for others. In such a scenario, the public casualties may be unconsciously regarded as collateral damage. In the past we had a situation where cigarette companies had 'experts' who defended the position that cigarettes did not cause cancer. Also, many food industries will have their 'experts' to defend their products regardless of the illness associated with their products. It also goes without saying that those involved in cancer research and treatment – including the scientists and doctors who develop and use chemotherapy drugs, will defend their positions. It is in your interest is to decide if their approach is still credible after their overseeing more than a hundred years of research. In this long span of time their activities have produced no cure but a constant increase in cancer death rates, to the current rate of over eight million deaths per annum. *No other industry in the world would be allowed to continue operating, and remain largely unchallenged, if it failed to deliver its objective after such a long time!*

There is a simple and easy way to settle this issue. There has to be an extensive trial that involves a radical change in a cancer victim's lifestyle and diet, with a comparison of the result with those who rely only on conventional chemo and radiation treatment. The information I have presented is the result of what I have gathered through my research. It is also based on my knowledge and experience, and the collective experiences and knowledge of others who have embraced the healing power of our bodies, the natural healing powers of Nature and its ability to restore the body to its natural balance. These are people who believe in and practise naturopathic medicine. In the final analysis it comes down to a simple but important difference in approach to the present 'scorched-earth' approach of allopathic medicine.

You've read earlier where the *Daily Express* newspaper declared that scientists have made "a very exciting 'breakthrough'" regarding the positive effect that oxygen has on cancer cells. It is instructional to note that the 'breakthrough' was not based on the effect of a drug on cancer. It means that now conventional science is on the same page as where the naturopaths have always been. However, their 'weapon' of choice still remains the usage of harmful chemotherapy drugs and radiation treatment whilst the naturopathic approach is simply to eliminate the causes of cancer and nourish the body with life giving nutrients such a oxygen, vitamins, minerals and herbs.

The naturopathic approach involves the following:

- The elimination of all meats including fish, and animal based foods such as milk and dairy products
- The elimination of all refined carbohydrates
- The elimination of all processed foods
- The elimination of all fried foods
- The elimination of salt (a preservative, not a food)
- The elimination of all sugars (a preservative, not a food).
- The elimination of all types of alcohol (listed as a poison in all chemistry books)
- The elimination of vinegar (a poison; not a food)
- A diet of raw fruits, vegetable and nuts – these can be prepared as juices
- Herbs that are known to carry oxygen to cells
- The use of alkaline water
- Regular, non-stressful, aerobic type of exercises – walking, cycling, etc.

This would in effect be an extensive *non-clinical* trial, as it would not be conducted in a lab. Such a trial would run parallel with, but in comparison to, those being treated in the conventional way. It would demonstrate which approach is more effective. If the approach that is being advocated by this book proves to be effective, we would have a situation where millions of lives would be saved now and in the future.

This would not only have an effect solely on cancer, it would also have an effect on all the other major diseases. Most importantly, it would revolutionize the thinking of many in terms of the way they view Nature, the science of foods, and the science of their body.

If this type of knowledge is adequately taught in our educational institutions and widely publicized, we could experience a global enlightenment of the healing powers of our body. There would be a global consciousness of the effectiveness of our body in defending us against, and curing us of disease if it is fed food substances that are compatible with its own science. From this we would get close to a desired goal: a lot more people will develop a culture of eating to live instead of living to eat, and this will lead to a massive reduction in cancer and other major non-communicable diseases.

I suggest that this non-clinical trial would create the same dynamic, as did the use of oranges, lemons and limes to cure and prevent the dreaded scurvy during the mid eighteenth century. The lessons surrounding the cure of scurvy could be applied to cancer and disease prevention in general. It is an opportunity to demonstrate that we can learn from history. As the saying goes, "Those who don't learn from history are doomed to repeat it." Yet the lessons surrounding scurvy are also an example of our not learning from history. Apparently, the first written account of a disease likely to be scurvy comes from the Ebers papyrus which has been dated to 1500 BC Egypt. The Ebers papyrus not only diagnosed scurvy, but prescribed that victims of scurvy be treated with onions, a common source of vitamin C. So, the tens of thousands who died from scurvy could have been saved by applying knowledge that had been acquired nearly two thousand years prior to the 'new' experience of the disease!

We have a situation where Nature has demonstrated that it can correct a life-ending problem with one of its undiluted products: oranges or lemons. So why would the use of Nature's unprocessed nutrients as a solution to life-ending diseases appears to be a strange idea to many? Part of the answer has to be the widespread absence of historical, nutritional knowledge, such as the case of the story of scurvy.

We've carried out many massive drugs trials for all sorts of diseases. In the case of cancer, the best that we've come up with are drugs that harm and kill. The one thing we haven't done is to conduct massive food and herbs trials. Many people do not have other people's interest at heart. Why would this not apply to governments? They are made up of people. Governments, who are to represent the will of the people, may not always act in their best interest. An example is the unsolicited addition of fluoride to human drinking water. Can we rely on them, therefore, to act in our best interest in terms of encouraging such trials?

The cancer industry is so huge and has so many layers of self-interest, and so many ingrained attitudes, that it is going to take a unique blend of interests with influence enough to spark a change. We need people with no self-interest, but with great influence, to put the alternative, naturopathic, case under the spotlight, and cause the American and other western governments to examine the evidence concerning cancer. All the doctors and scientists who have exposed the harm of chemotherapy would be ideal candidates to form a nucleus to lobby for change.

I mentioned the American government because, as far as I am aware, they are the only government to pass a *Conquest of Cancer Act,* with a mandate for eliminating cancer. Secondly, America holds a unique position of global influence, and this means they could initiate change faster than any other country. The world needs a change real fast. We need people who can put the cancer industry on the spot, so that their actions will demonstrate if they were, or are, sincere in their desire to eliminate cancer.

You've read where Dr. Warburg's discovery is now 'a new breakthrough'. Yet, nearly a hundred years ago he quoted Max Planck out of frustration of the lack of acceptance of his ideas. Hopefully we are not in a situation where the following quote is still true:

A new scientific truth does not triumph by convincing opponents and making them see the light, but rather because its opponents eventually die, and a new generation grows up that is familiar with it. –Scientific Autobiography and other papers by Max Planck

Unfortunately for the world, even though we have had several generations of doctors, the fixation on drug therapy is stronger than ever. So, even after arriving full circle, back to Dr. Warburg's discovery, the approach towards cancer treatment remains practically the same. We owe it to millions of people who will live if they become aware of the dangers of chemotherapy and the merits of the alternative, naturopathic approach. We also owe it to millions of those who are yet to be born, who will be victims of this *drugs to treat symptoms* culture, if nothing is done.

We owe it to our own self-interest to promote the link between food and cancer. Even though there is the risk that, just like people knowing the dangers of smoking and still smoke, many will still ignore such advice. However, some *will* heed the advice. It is in our self-interest to promote this link because of the enormous brain drain that cancer and other diseases are causing. There is also the devastation in families, caused by the unquantifiable loss of the emotional, social and financial support provided previously by the member who has been killed by cancer. And of course, what affects the family affects the community and, ultimately, the nation.

If all of the information in this book becomes a debate, the objective should not be to win; the objective should be to expose the truth. The arguments cannot have financial considerations, because the value of human life should always supersede such considerations.

The prediction that new cases of cancer will almost double by 2050 has to be taken seriously. Yet, this prediction could be conservative. I say this because of noted increases in alcohol consumption in the United Kingdom and other countries in recent years, and the constant growth of the junk food industry.

At present, the seven or more million people who die annually of cancer has not caused an international panic sufficient enough to result in an examination of the current cancer treatment industry. The question is, what if the number of deaths reaches twenty million or fifty million per annum? Would this cause an examination of the cancer industry and its method of treatment? I don't think that the numbers, by themselves, will cause such an examination. This is largely because the majority of the world's population will remain uninformed about the causes and nature of cancer, if we make a judgement based upon what has happened so far.

The cancer industry is locked into a 'drug-to-treat' paradigm, and regards itself as being en route to a valid solution. So I believe a massive increase in the numbers of cancer deaths is very probable. I think the best way to stop this likelihood is the global edification of people. It is the awareness of massive numbers of people that will provide a sufficient groundswell of opinion that can demand that the cancer industry changes its approach.

The cancer industry has far too much self-interest and is locked too deeply in its lucrative drugs-treatment paradigm for it to change without being forcefully prompted. Hopefully this book will be successful enough in raising global awareness, and the information I have shared can become the basis upon which the cancer industry and its methods of treatment are closely examined, challenged, and reformed.

Those who are suffering from cancer and their loved ones will not directly benefit from a debate that is promulgated on 'winning the argument'. They want a solution now.

When my late aunt, Yvonne, was suffering from cancer, I suffered the greatest frustration and anguish because of my realisation that she was locked into believing in a system that had failed her before. I had an enormous feeling of helplessness from the realisation that I couldn't help her, and this feeling was eventually tinged with a sense that her death was inevitable.

My effort to introduce her to an alternative approach had started as soon as she was diagnosed with cancer two years prior to her death. I had very little success. She was a retired nurse, therefore her belief in the allopathic approach to cancer treatment was very strong. Her training and respect for her profession make her too inflexible to even look at an alternative solution. I don't blame her because those charged with informing us about health and well being have done an excellent job in ensuring that the allopathic approach is believed by the masses to be the only viable choice.

I hope you, the reader, will accept that it is only if the use of natural remedies and dietary and lifestyle changes are rigorously tried as a solution, and the results published, that we can sincerely claim that we have done all we can to eliminate the scourge we call cancer.

CPSIA information can be obtained at www.ICGtesting.com
Printed in the USA
BVOW08s0453230616

453019BV00002B/109/P